Resentment in History

Resentment in History

Marc Ferro

Translated by Steven Rendall

polity

First published in French as *Le ressentiment dans l'Histoire* © Odile Jacob, April 2007

This English edition © Polity Press 2010

Polity Press
65 Bridge Street
Cambridge CB2 1UR, UK

Polity Press
350 Main Street
Malden, MA 02148, USA

Ouvrage publié avec le concours du ministère Français de la Culture – Centre national du livre

Published with the assistance of the French Ministry of Culture – National Centre for the Book

ISBN-13: 978-0-7456-4686-2 (hardback)
ISBN-13: 978-0-7456-4687-9 (paperback)

A catalogue record for this book is available from the British Library.

Typeset in 11 on 13 pt Sabon
by Toppan Best-set Premedia Limited
Printed and bound in Great Britain by MPG Books Group Limited, Bodmin, Cornwall

The publisher has used its best endeavours to ensure that the URLs for external websites referred to in this book are correct and active at the time of going to press. However, the publisher has no responsibility for the websites and can make no guarantee that a site will remain live or that the content is or will remain appropriate.

For further information on Polity, visit our website: www.politybooks.com

Contents

1

The Enslaved and the Persecuted: An Age-Old Resentment

In Antiquity, the fate of the enslaved and persecuted, the first rebels in history, leads us down an unusual path. In the Greco-Roman world, non-free foreigners – most were prisoners of war – and natives were often thrown into slavery because they could not pay their debts. The Greeks established many procedures for freeing slaves, however freed slaves did not become full citizens, but rather metics who could be enslaved again if they showed an aggressive ingratitude – which testifies to their resentment. Among those who worked in the mines, a communal consciousness might appear. It took political form in the slave revolt in Laurium in 429, during the Peloponnesian war. The slaves' sole thought was to run away to recover their freedom.

After the revolts that had broken out in Sicily, where opulence and poverty existed side by side in an ostentatious manner, a spectacular uprising took place. It was led by a Thracian named Spartacus who in 73 BCE was able to convince the gladiators at the school in Capua that their condition was unworthy of them and that they should put an end to it. He was able to flee with seventy of the gladiators. Having defeated the troops sent to dislodge him from the slopes of Mt Vesuvius, Spartacus was joined by rural slaves and shepherds who had lost their lands. His army of 70,000 men laid waste to Italy. He was an educated, reflective man who wanted his troops to make their way back to the lands where they had been born, their original countries. But the Senate, terrified, put six legions under the command of Crassus, who finally defeated Spartacus and his gladiators, and crucified 6,000 prisoners along the Appian Way.

If resentment against cruel masters who forced them to participate in these ignominious spectacles aroused this kind of revolt, the condition of slaves was soon exploited by political agitators who used them to seize power. That was what Sergius Catilina, that handsome, young, silver-tongued patrician who was seeking the consulate did. He came from an impoverished noble family and had gotten rich by buying up at cheap prices the property of people that Rome had proscribed. After spending some time in Africa, where he was accused of misappropriating public funds, he gathered around him a group of déclassés, unemployed rustics, and henchmen. His program? Land reform and debt relief. He proclaimed himself head of the party of the impoverished, the general of the poor. In the Senate, he proposed the theory that "the state consists of two bodies, one weak with a head that is not very strong, the other strong but without a head." He would be the latter's head. When he didn't hesitate to commit murder, his former allies, Crassus and Caesar, disowned him. Through his eloquence, Cicero was able to discredit him: *Quousque tandem abutere, Catilina, patientia nostra?* ("How long, at last, O Catiline, will you abuse our patience?") He was ultimately defeated and killed in combat.

As for other subjects and citizens of Greco-Roman Antiquity, including freedmen, it was envy that exuded their resentment toward the powerful. The diffuse hostility that the latter aroused had less to do with their wealth itself, as Paul Veyne has shown, than with their display of it. Showing themselves munificent toward the civic collectivity was certainly not sufficient to attenuate the wealthy's presumption. "You gave me a show," one of Petronius's heroes says, "but I applauded you; add it up – I spent more than I got, one hand washes the other." The donor's generosity is paid in advance by the social distance he enjoys. The gift, the generosity, attenuate hardly at all the envy, one of the sources of resentment. In the Mediterranean region, this is a centuries-old way of seeing things: "You were able to get our money before you became generous," seventeenth-century peasants told a Spanish notable who had just made a large donation to the church.[1] And since the

[1] Quoted by J. Caro Baroja in *Honour and Shame: The Values of Mediterranean Society*.

Middle Ages, gratitude has seemed all the less justified because the generosity of the elites has become a requirement made by the church or by its bishops.

Since the Middle Ages, envy has appeared only if the inequality that aroused it disappears. It is not directed against the eternal pomp of the church. When it is not someone's personal property but his inaccessible genius that is envied, resentment can lead to murder, as it did in the case of the assassination of Caesar by Brutus, whose love for the Republic was probably only one of his motives. Closer to our own time, a figurative murder was committed by Salieri, who had been traumatized by the unimaginable gifts of the young Mozart, whose career he followed with increasing resentment. Still closer to us, when he discovered the incomparable Charlie Chaplin, the comedian W. C. Fields declared: "He's the best ballet dancer that ever lived and if I get a good chance I'll kill him with my bare hands."

The era of Christianity

With the advent of Christianity, the divine was no longer identified with the order of the world or with a powerful figure, but with a being as weak as anyone, Christ, and this makes everyone his equal, provided that one believes in him. To be sure, nature is not egalitarian, but for Christians, everyone is equal in dignity. Thus appears the idea of the rights of man, and also the idea of a universal community beyond the practices of the various peoples of the Roman Empire. Religion requires one to have confidence in Christ's teaching, in other words, not to imagine that one can think for oneself. For those whom life had mistreated, the slaves and other persecuted groups, this reversal comes after a long, powerless wait; then there is an inversion of values for those victims who had nourished hopes of some revenge against their oppressors, but in vain. Christianity promises them this revenge: "since I cannot take revenge on the powerful, I count on God: is it not written that "the last shall be the first," that "Blessed are they that suffer persecution for justice's sake, for theirs is the kingdom of heaven"?

Although ancient society regarded slavery as natural, the Christian church's position seems ambiguous. On the one hand, it desired that slavery be made less cruel, but on the other it did not free its own slaves and did not allow them to enter the clergy.

Moreover, it thought that freeing slaves would decrease God's patrimony. St Augustine and Isidore of Seville (fourth and sixth centuries) proclaimed the legitimacy and necessity of slavery, conceived as a providential means of redeeming humanity through penitence. But at the same time, proclaiming that "all men are brothers" and offering fugitive slaves asylum in its churches, where they might be freed, Christianity humanized this servitude. Slaves were baptized and thus stripped of their rags. By asserting their love for the poor, by using a simple and direct language, by making their action visible, the bishops were to found their authority on this aid to the unfortunate, and thus supplied something that met many demands. The church created a new sensibility: in this religion, morals are more important than rites.

Then a kind of ambivalent society was created, many of the Empire's subjects leading a double life, as it were: one life that followed the precepts of the Apostles, and another that obeyed the state's orders, while refusing to commit certain acts, such as fighting wars: "Blessed are the peacemakers: for they shall be called the children of God." The first people martyred for refusing to serve in the armies died in the third century, according to Tertullian. Thus there was a divorce between obedience to the law which, until Constantine, considered Christianity a crime, and a society that was gradually Christianized from bottom to top, finally reaching Maria, the wife of the emperor Commodus.

Christianity demanded that slavery be made less cruel. From the moment that the Emperor Constantine himself became a Christian in 325, the state was animated by the concern for justice and humanity: the protection of the humble against the arbitrariness of the powerful, the prohibition on separating a slave from his family when he was sold, the prohibition of gladiatorial battles, and so on. But at the same time, whereas the fate of the unfortunate became easier to bear, the first two *Letters* issued by the Christian emperor after his conversion stigmatized those who, after having crucified Jesus, did not adopt the "universal religion," the Jews, and those who contested its foundations, the heretics, such as Donatus and later on, Arius. The church's resentment was henceforth directed against them. But for a few centuries, it was directed more against the heretics than against the Jews, who were reproached only for being half-Christians.

Emphasizing that the slave revolt in Antiquity began when resentment became creative and secreted a true reaction – revolt, the Christian religion offering compensation through imaginary vengeance, Nietzsche and then Scheler revealed a structure whose persistence should be investigated. The two authors do not deduce the same effects from this structure. For Nietzsche, the effects are perverse, because man thereby loses his sovereignty; for Scheler, they are fortunate, because man finds in them his freedom.

When the persecuted becomes the persecutor

One of the most spectacular features of the change that occurred when the Roman Emperor Constantine converted to Christianity in 312 was this reversal: the persecuted became the persecutor. Up to that point, the Christian had been the victim of the imperial laws, religious crime being regarded as the equivalent of civil disobedience. The Christians (or Jews) were not punished because of their beliefs, but because they did not fully participate in the life of the city, for example by refusing to make sacrifices in honor of the emperor or the official gods. Or else by behaving in a hostile manner when a monarch passed by, which under Caligula led the prefect Flaccus to order a massacre of the Jews. Thus, in a work on persecution in Antiquity, Marie-Françoise Baslez records several dozen actions against Christians carried out by the authorities without recording those that were directed against them along with the Jews, astrologers, Chaldeans, and so on, or those that targeted the Jews during the second destruction of Jerusalem in 70 CE.

If it is difficult to evaluate the number of Christians who died, some of them as martyrs, it is thought that, for example, during the persecutions of 300–303, in a single year the province of Africa had about 200 martyrs, Egypt 144, and Palestine 44. But not all the dead and persecuted were martyrs. Above all, the Christians, seen as disturbing public order, lived in a permanent insecurity fed by the fear of anything that might trigger persecution, whatever its origin. This fear was nourished by natural catastrophes, fires, urban violence, and even the ruler's irritation or anxiety. In *De Mortibus Persecutorum* ("On the death of the persecutors"), Lactantius, the "Christians' Cicero," describes the origins of the campaign of persecution launched by Diocletian in 299–301.

Diocletian was sojourning in Antioch while he prepared an expedition against the Sassanid Persians. Worried, in accord with the most ancient Italic laws he consulted the haruspex. The entrails did not speak; the gods refused to give a sign as to the outcome of the campaign. A serious threat thus hung over the emperor's projects. His official haruspex attributed the gods' silence to the presence of Christians in the Imperial guard, who were supposed to have crossed themselves to desacralize the scene that they were witnessing. They were betrayed and then, according to Lactantius, Diocletian, in the grip of a mystical anxiety, decided to eliminate Christians from his army, including the Manicheans. The persecution continued until early 303; it was planned to demolish churches, destroy books, confiscate sacred vessels, and prohibit meetings; Christian notables were to be deprived of their civil rights, members of the Imperial household cast into slavery, and the leaders of the church imprisoned. But by the end of the year, because the prisons were overflowing, an amnesty was declared, on the condition that the offenders made a public sacrifice. Then came the massacre of St Irene, and a group of Christian women in Thessalonika, for having kept forbidden books and other objects.

How should we account for the turnaround a few decades later, in which the resentment of these Christian victims transformed them into persecutors, not of the state and the emperor, since the latter had in the meantime converted, but of the pagans, the Jews, and still more of Christians like themselves?

We will come back to the Jews – defined as deicides – later on, but let us note here that before Constantine converted in 330, they had already been victims, along with the Christians, of common persecutions and of common measures of clemency, despite the conflicts that had already occurred between the two groups. The transformation of persecuted Christians into Christians who persecuted Christians is a problem. Marie-Françoise Baslez accounts for this by arguing that the Christians represented only one faction among others in the city, an outside threat to its functioning, whereas henceforth it was within the church that factions were to be found. One of the first examples is that of the adepts of Bishop Donatus, who would not accept that *lapsi* – that is, those who during the persecutions had become apostates by agreeing to burn incense before the altar of the pagan gods or by turning sacred books over to the authorities – should remain Christians or be re-baptized. These "pure men" thought the emperor had nothing to do with Christianity. For their part, they resisted the persecution; among them were martyrs who had, as much as those who resisted, set an example as imitators of Christ, and they fought for their religion, like missionaries. But the church persecuted these Donatists because, especially in Africa, most Christians had denied their faith; now they wanted to return to their religion and all those who had failed to do their duty could not be rejected. So the Donatists became victims of persecution. In this example, one of the first, we find a mixture of resentment, the requirement of purity, and perhaps also a whiff of identity politics, in this case in reaction to Romanization.

The Jews and the heretics, in the Middle Ages and afterward

Deicides responsible for the crucifixion of Christ, the Jews traumatized the Christians. They had already aroused the ire of the Roman emperor by refusing to sacrifice to the cult of his person. But in the early Empire the emperors, despairing of assimilating them, had granted them privileges taking into account the demands of their religion. This changed with the conversion of the Empire to Christianity: if Constantine simply stigmatized the Jews, his son Constans took steps hostile to them that had been drawn from the arsenal earlier built up against the factions. At the same time, he forbade pagans to celebrate sacrifices. Things took a different turn with Julian the Apostate. For him, Jehovah was merely an ethnic god, worthy of respect. He wanted to defuse the Jews' hatred for Rome and especially to refute Jesus' prophecy that the destruction of the Temple in Jerusalem was definitive.

This recognition of Judaism reawakened Christian fanaticism. In response, it was the Jews' turn to burn churches, and a first flare-up of massacres resulted. With Theodosius, there was a return to persecution; in 384 he confirmed the prohibition on Jews owning Christian slaves. In addition, he stipulated that marriages between Jews and Christians would be punished as adulterous. But he made it explicit that no law banned "the Jewish sect." It remains that for the church, the persecution of the enemies of

Christ was a sign of identity, a way of differentiating itself from them, since the Jews could not acknowledge that Christ, because he had been crucified, could be a god, since for them God incarnated omnipotence. For the church this sign of identity was supposed to lead Christians to establish the status of the Jew in this Christian world. "Do not kill them for fear that my people might forget, but let your Power drive them away and bring them down, that is, demean them." The inferiority of the Jews was supposed to be made constantly perceptible in order all the more to valorize Christian identity.

However, although the church for several centuries feared the competition and the influence of Judaism and called for the separation of the Christians from the Jews, it did not try to eliminate them. Around the twelfth century, we nonetheless see anti-Judaism become more radically hostile and internalized, especially in popular milieus, as the church increasingly regulated the lives of Christians and multiplied edicts, notably concerning sexuality. The impure body of the Jew who lived apart threatened to contaminate the Christian body. But what do these Jews do, anyway, remaining among themselves and clinging to their customs? The worse fantasies well up from their tendency to keep to themselves, gradually arousing distrust, jealousy, and hatred.[2] Up to that point, manifestations of anti-Judaism had been relatively rare, as were all persecutions. Granting the Jews, alongside the prohibitions of which they were the object, the right to lend at interest aroused a resurgence of popular hostility, the church emphasizing that "lending at interest, Jews could be regarded as enemies." They also harmed the state treasury by charging interest that diminished taxable revenues. And "it is Judaism that commanded them to want to do harm." An accusation that was not made against the Lombards, who were not Jews, and other moneylenders in the Christian world. But it was on the basis of the Gregorian reforms, and still more on that of the church's control over the Western monarchies, that the Jews were "ghettoized," distinguishing themselves all the more from other groups by their continuing adherence to their traditions. Thus, they were the first victims of the Crusades. They were accused of ritual murders, of

[2] Alain Boureau.

having poisoned the wells even during the 1348 plague, in short of desiring the death of Christianity.

The impossibility of taking revenge produced a resentment that the church maintained as it consolidated its authority and the king became its eldest son. In France, for example, good King Louis, the "king of moderation and wisdom," told Joinville that "when a layman hears a Jew speak ill of Christian law, he should defend it in no way other than with his sword, which he should thrust into his adversary's belly as far as it will go."

Generation after generation, the church's teaching perpetuated this resentment, which was reinforced by other components, both in the West and in the Orthodox countries of the East. In Spain, it was the crusading spirit against Islam and the Jews that won out, whereas the Mediterranean countries, Greece and Italy, where the pope reigned, escaped to some extent the most aggressive forms of hatred against the Jews. For instance, in Languedoc and Provence, where the early development of Christian commerce and credit had made the Jews less distinct from the rest of society, people certainly participated in the church's anti-Judaism but seldom accused Jews of ritual murders, the first accusation being made in Valréas in 1247. But in the rest of Europe, as Léon Poliakov has shown, the fate of the Jews grew steadily worse, whether following a famine like that of 1315, which led to the Shepherds' Crusade, directed not against the Saracens but against the Jews, especially in Aquitaine, or following the plague of 1348, especially in Germany, where "Jew holes" (*Judenlachen*) were numerous.

Since that time, "Jewish devils" have been commemorated at Easter time in San Fratello, a mountain village near Palermo. Each part of the village participates, some representing the Passion, others Jews disguised as devils. The latter came charging in, disturbing the cortege and generally causing mischief. These tragedies accelerated the relegation of the Jews into ghettos, their expulsion, their turning inward upon themselves. As Erasmus put it: "If a good Christian detests Jews, then we're all good Christians."

In the West, the English Jews' response to the staging of *The Merchant of Venice* in 1596, which has been studied by Jean Clavreul, allows us to see the source of the resentment, not on the part of Christians, but on the part of Jews, and how it can be reduced when the latter are confronted by a situation they perceive as hostile. Shakespeare's play is not solely about anti-Judaism. We recall that a rich merchant, Antonio, has to borrow money from his arch-enemy, Shylock, a Jewish usurer. The latter agrees to lend him the money at no interest, asking only that he sign, as security for his debt, a note giving the lender the right to take a pound of his debtor's flesh in the event that he does not repay the money. Antonio accepts, thinking it is a joke, but when the debt comes due and he has paid nothing, Shylock takes his revenge, invoking the legal power of the state incarnated by the Doge to ensure that the contract is respected. Powerless to avenge himself for the affronts he has had to endure because money lending is the only profession he is allowed to practice, Shylock feeds on his expectations, and he thinks his resentment is finally about to be satisfied by vengeance. Except that an unexpected dramatic turnaround finally deprives him of it. Another law is discovered that forbids shedding Christian blood, and for having intended to violate it, Shylock is condemned to convert to Christianity.

The interest of this story resides in the fact that on coming out of the theater, the Jewish spectators, far from criticizing its anti-Jewish nature, expressed favorable opinions about it. First of all because it proved that Jews were more interested in respecting contracts than in the money they might bring in. And especially, because instead of being the victims of laws of exclusion, they were at last treated like other citizens of Venice. They were no longer simply different from other people, they could be both like others and retain their traditions. Rooted in this land, their refusal to convert was nonetheless to condemn them to live in a ghetto, that of Venice, which thus became one of the first ghettos in Europe.

Two centuries after the expulsion of the Jews from Spain and their scattering from Bordeaux to Amsterdam, from Italy to Greece and the Maghreb, the idea of a Jewish nationality emerged in central and especially eastern Europe as a reaction as much to secularization as to anti-Judaism. This twofold threat turned into a creative power, the Jews valorizing their situation and taking pride in the fact that without a state, without land, dispersed, their identity had persisted, and thanks to religion alone, a unique example that the Arab historian Ibn Khaldun had once celebrated.

The Zionist project, the idea of a return to the Holy Land, emerged in Yiddish-speaking areas after the pogroms in Russia, Poland, and the Ukraine in 1881 that followed the assassination of the "liberating" Czar Alexander II by a terrorist – who was, moreover, not a Jew. Other militants, more to the West and South, were mostly of the view, despite the rise of anti-Semitism, especially in France and Germany, that the memory of a land of origin was the sole bond, and a slender one at that, that united all Jews and that consequently they should remain citizens of the countries where they resided. With the rise of Nazism and the Fascist movements of Central and Eastern Europe, Jews, who had become pariahs in many countries, were won over to the Zionist idea of a return to the Promised Land.

A recent pogrom, a heritage of anti-Judaism

10 July 1941. The massacre of the Jews of Jedwabne in Poland is certainly associated with the Wehrmacht's invasion of this part of the country, which was formerly Russian. But the massacre was carried out by Poles, by them alone, and the Wehrmacht hadn't asked them to do anything. Sixteen hundred Jews lived in this small town, and only seven survived, having been saved by a Polish woman who lived nearby. All the rest were clubbed to death by their neighbors, dashed with gasoline and set afire, or drowned in the marshes.

"It was time to deal with the people who crucified Christ," one of the killers said afterward, in 1949. "Yes, we were taught that in school." He confirmed that the Poles had acted willingly, the Germans helping them and laughing at the spectacle of these atrocities and taking photos. The local priest, upon whom a few of the wretched victims had called for help, refused to intervene.

Jan T. Gross, the author of *The Neighbors*, tells us that all these Poles – young and old, men and women – ran eagerly to see the victims whom Polish murderers had killed with clubs, as if they wanted to witness a horrible "miracle." Being taught that the Jews had crucified Jesus was the first wound that these Poles had received in their early infancy. Passed on from generation to generation, it had aroused a desire for vengeance and that vengeance had finally been taken. "We were taught that in school ..."

In fact, after the adoption of the "March Constitution" in 1921, the Catholic Church received ninety percent of the subsidies granted in Poland to schools in which religious instruction was a the rule. In 1936, in a *Pastoral Letter* the primate of Poland accused Jews of being the root of all evils. This was a far cry from the happy period when, protected by the monarch, the Jews had obtained from Sigismund II Augustus a charter of protection on condition that they paid their taxes. With the partitions of Poland in the eighteenth century, there was a resumption of the persecutions the Catholic Church had encouraged by contesting the laws of protection that the Jews had obtained and threatening to punish those who had crucified Jesus unless they converted. Except that in school they had not been told that Jesus was a Jew ...

This massacre was the harbinger of the systematic extermination that the Nazi regime was to perpetrate, made easier by the presence of the Wehrmacht, but exclusively popular and spontaneous in origin. This pogrom was the precise and pure expression of a millennial resentment. "We were taught that in school."

But this was true in Germany as well, and not only in school, insofar as the whole culture implanted and maintained hostility to the Jews: catechism, children's family upbringing, sermons, and so on. Onto this anti-Judaism was grafted an anti-Semitism that arose in part from the democratization of Western societies after the French Revolution. Democracy allowed Jews, who had become citizens, to spread throughout society, and henceforth to engage in different activities – the arts, literature, politics, and so on; they were no longer limited to little trades or money dealing, with the state or not. Perceived as competitors, they now found themselves both inside and outside society insofar as many of them retained part or all of their traditions, to the point that the idea that they were a race could arise. Thus a more or less racist anti-Semitism could be added to the original anti-Judaism that the Jews' activity as money lenders had produced for centuries.

However, Jeanne Favret-Saada's work shows that this description of a transition from anti-Judaism to anti-Semitism is schematic. Rather than seeing in it a succession of two phenomena, she shows that the cultural heritage of anti-Judaism can survive in the form of an "outlier" (*butte-témoin*) in the midst of a society that has been transformed and that partly acknowledges its anti-

Semitism. Her argument is based on the Passion Play that has been performed in Oberammergau in Bavaria since 1634, and that became internationally famous in the nineteenth century, drawing several hundreds of thousands of participants, many of whom came from the Americas. In 1901, this Passion Play was accused of being an anti-Semitic celebration, whereas at that time the term "anti-Judaism" would have been just as appropriate, even though the fusion of the two feelings had already taken place. After the Second World War, American Jewish associations and other, non-Jewish groups decried these features of the Passion Play. To be sure, since Vatican II, the Catholic Church has expressed sincere repentance, making it possible to revise the formulas of catechisms and sermons. At the fourth session of Vatican II (1965), Paul VI declared that "The Church recognizes and accepts its Jewish origin; the Jews, our brothers, are not responsible for the death of Jesus Christ on the Cross."

But, for all that, there was no acknowledgment of the church's past relationships with the Jews. So that in the name of a tradition to be respected, except for a few details, the Oberammergaus could continue the anti-Jewish spirit of their Passion Play. The

Archives du 7ᵉ Art-Photo12.com

The Passion, a depository of resentment.

spectacle was in fact constructed in such a way that the participants could not imagine – any more than the Poles at Jedwabne
– that Jesus was also a Jew, and this exacerbated their resentment
toward those who had crucified him. For their part, despite the
repentance expressed by John XXIII in the Holy Land, the Jews
of the Diaspora and of Israel retained a strong resentment against
the papacy, whose behavior with regard to the Nazis remains an
indelible stain. But if Pius XII's stubborn silence during the genocide, clearly pointed out in Cardinal Spellman's report in May
1942, is explained both by his fervor for Germany and his hostility to Bolshevism and "Marxo-democracies," the wound remains.
It has remained painful even if people other than the Jews –
notably the Serbs who were massacred by Hungarian and Albanian fascists during World War II – have been victims of these
crimes and this complicitous silence.

Since then, the Jews' resentment has been reactivated on many
occasions, notably by the beatification of Pope Pius IX, who called
Jews "dogs," a decision presented as an internal matter within the
Catholic Church, "which in no way injures Catholics' reconciliation with them." As for those responsible for the genocide or their
accomplices – like the Vichy government – resentment against
German leaders from Brandt to Schröder has calmed because they
have constantly expressed repentance for the tragedy and thus
shown that their country's guilt still torments them.

It is not clear, however, that middle-aged Germans of the middle
or lower classes share this attitude. Recalling their former victories and the glory they have recovered through their economy, they
rarely feel repentance; they cultivate confidence in their strength
and live without guilt. Thus in 1958 a German businessman told
Jean Amery, a concentration camp survivor, "that the German
people felt no bitterness toward the Jewish people: he found evi-
dence enough for this in the generous reparations policy con-
ducted by the government, and to which the state of Israel paid
tribute ... Having suffered so much at Stalingrad and elsewhere,
Germans held no grudge against resistance fighters or Jews. Hadn't
they all been victims? [*sic*]."

It was then, and then only, that Jean Amery, a Belgian, a
member of the Resistance, and a Jew, felt resentment again. Confronted by the arrogance of the new Germany, he felt alone and
powerless again. Other bruising blows were to follow. According

to the *Frankfurter Rundschau*, the construction of the Holocaust Memorial in Berlin was entrusted in part to the company that during the war produced Zyklon B gas. According to the Christian-Democratic deputy Martin Hohmann on 14 November 2003, "Germans have never been treated leniently. The dominant clique of historians and politicians opposes that with all its strength ... forgetting that Jews have also committed crimes, that it was Jewish Bolsheviks that traumatized Hitler." We will return to this myth.

A crusade against Christian heretics

For Catholicism, heresy had always been the main enemy. It took more than a century to formulate a single Catholic credo. At the beginning of the fifth century, St Augustine counted 88 heresies. "A heretic is someone who is not only in error but persists in it." Starting with the period of Constantine, those who rejected the Church Fathers' authority were persecuted by the state, and a few centuries later heresy was defined as a crime of *lèse-majesté*. These heretics questioned the reality of the Trinity, denounced the pope's temporal power, or saw the pope as the Antichrist, but above all they condemned the church's corruption and demanded a return to the purity of its origins. They wanted to purge the church of the pleasures of the flesh, of the love of money, and of power.

So long as these heretics were scattered, the pope and the bishops could combat them, but when they got organized and acquired a territorial base, the ecclesiastical hierarchy sensed danger. They were confronted by the Albigensians in Languedoc and the Cathars, who, following in the footsteps of the Waldensians in the valley of the Po a century earlier, preached asceticism and poverty. Innocent III's crusade against them was the first launched by a pope against Christians.

Since Count Raymond VI of Toulouse, a tolerant ruler and a friend of the troubadours, paid no attention to their admonishments, the bishops appealed to the pope, who called upon Simon de Montfort, who was then in the service of the Capetians, to crush the heresy. It was on this occasion that, after having besieged Beziers, the abbé general of Citeaux and papal legate is said to have cried: "Kill them all, God will recognize his own" (1209). This wound has never completely healed.

The Albigensian Crusade allowed King Louis VIII to complete his conquest of Languedoc and to integrate it into the royal domain. This forced integration led to an identity-based reaction on the part of the people in southern France against the northern part of the kingdom. It had seen waves of conquerors of all origins in the guise of crusaders, called "Teutonic knights" on the inscription of a small cemetery in Auvezines, a village in southwestern France near Revel, where ten thousand of their victims are said to have been massacred. A dream of imaginary vengeance, resentment engraved in stone. The resentment aroused by the repression of the Cathars was ultimately replaced in Aquitaine by the resentment felt by the Tuchins, peasants who had revolted against excessively heavy taxes levied by King Jean (known as "the good"), who thus displayed his ingratitude to them, though it was they who, when the region was occupied by the English, had shown their loyalty to the king of France. Then in the sixteenth century the Ordinance of Villers-Cotterêts issued by Francois I forbade the use of the Occitan language – their language – in administrative documents.

From anti-heresy to anti-Protestantism

The accumulation of these aggressions accounts for the fact that the Protestant message received a more favorable hearing in southern France than elsewhere, because there a certain anti-clericalism had taken root as a consequence of other violent acts committed since the Inquisition. And when Louis XIV revoked the Edict of Nantes in 1685, he triggered a revolt in the Cévennes known as the "Camisard Rebellion."

Thus, from one end of its history to the other, from the stake at Montségur where 225 faithful Cathars were burned in 1244 to the dispersion of the "Synods of the Desert" in which pastors tried to keep the flame of Protestantism alive, Occitania felt itself to be the victim of both monarchical absolutism and Catholic absolutism, which were definitely associated with each other.

Up until the Revolution, Languedoc continued to be the province that showed the most bitterness against the monarchy. Jean Nicolas's calculations indicate that in Lower Languedoc alone, there were 839 rebellions, which puts the province of Languedoc as a whole ahead of Brittany (736) or the Île de France (808). In

1907, the image of the crusade returns with the agricultural crisis. The winegrowers refer to "the cruel selfishness of the beet growers in the North who are sacrificing the South, like worthy descendants of Simon de Montfort." On a banner we read: "Everybody following the banner of winegrowing, as in the time of the ancient crusade, our army camps at the foot of Carcassès. Noble cause, holy cause. Our ancestors fell like heroes to defend it. Winegrowers, my brothers, you will be worthy of them."

During the 1960s, the renaissance of the Occitan movement was seen from Toulouse to Tarascon, burning sparks appeared again in the Larzac after 1968 when the state tried to appropriate land to give it to the army. And today, it is from Millau, at the foot of the Larzac, that José Bové has launched his battle against the excesses of free-market economics. Thus here, too, it is a long-standing resentment that has led to the revalorization of an area's own culture against the vulgar violence of the North, from the art of the troubadours to the appearance of Frédéric Mistral's Félibrige movement in the nineteenth century, and the strengthening of a regional awareness.

One of the merits of Philippe Joutard's work on the Camisards was to show that in the Cévennes the oral tradition has preserved a certain sensitivity to this past. To be sure, since the eighteenth century, scholarly quarrels about interpretations have enlivened many debates between Catholics and Protestants. But beyond such reminiscences, this memory has remained a family memory passed on since 1702–1704 by word of mouth. It concerns the excruciating manifestation of a resentment that is expressed in various forms but is always directed against the centralizing state. Symbolically, Cévennes and Rouergue want to be lands of refuge and resistance, holding out a helping hand to many refugees and others who refused to participate in the STO (forced labor in Germany) during the Occupation and being home to numerous Resistance groups.

It was only with Malesherbes' edict of tolerance in 1787 that all Protestants in France could feel that they had been completely reintegrated into the national community. Their religion was officially recognized by Napoleon Bonaparte in 1802. Nonetheless, Catholics' resentment was revived in turn because after 1815 the Protestant church engaged in a certain proselytism. Historical scholarship was then booming, and brought up the subject of the "time of troubles" that we now call the "Wars of Religion." At the time, Montaigne had been keenly aware of what was happening, writing that "in the strife that is tearing France to pieces and dividing us into factions, each man labors to defend his cause – but even the best of them resort to dissimulation and lying." In truth, beyond the religious conflict over the interpretation of the Bible, the behavior of the clergy, and God knows what else, both sides targeted the royal power, the Protestants questioning its nature, and the Catholics condemning its growing independence from the Catholic Church and the pope.

Anti-Protestant polemics were revived in the nineteenth century, but in a different form. They had less to do with religious or governmental practices, which had been monarchical until 1848, imperial until 1871, and then republican, than with the identity of France as a nation, the eldest daughter of the Catholic Church for some people, and a daughter of the Revolution of 1789 for others. After the debacle of 1870–1871, the extreme right, led by Charles Maurras, resumed hateful diatribes against Protestants. Some newspapers, such as *Le Pays* and *La Délivrance*, maintained that Protestants were "foreigners within" who were taking part in a sort of conspiracy against the nation. Didn't their ideas, from Wycliff to Luther, come from countries that are France's enemies? Protestants, Maurras explained, constitute a state within the state, their cosmopolitanism is the precise opposite of national feeling. They privilege the individual and the universal to the detriment of the national community, Maurice Barrès added.

"Let the Protestants leave!" Émile Zola wrote in no uncertain terms in 1881. "They are colonizing the nation, perverting its soul, masses of them are engaged in secular education." Very small masses, we should note, since they constituted only two to three percent of the population. When a few of them became government ministers around 1880 – the engineer Freycinet and the diplomat Waddington – "they are everywhere," Maurras's *L'Action française* wrote. These are the same invectives that were soon directed against French-born Jews. This is the time of the trial of Captain Dreyfus, whose defenders were often Alsatians like himself, or Protestants – including Émile Zola, who had joined the camp of the defenders of the Rights of Man.

Now there was no more a Protestant conspiracy than there was a Jewish conspiracy such as was purely and simply invented by

DB © Universal/D.R.

The reciprocity of resentment: having been the victims of the Catholics, the Protestants burn Catholics in their turn.

the *Protocols of the Elders of Zion*, a counterfeit record of the 1897 congress of Zionists in which the latter are supposed to have worked out a plan for world domination – a false document written by the Czar's police. We can agree with the sociologists Bauberot and Zuber that between Catholics and Protestants in France, at the end of the First World War "hatred has been forgotten." But it remained under the surface and re-emerged during the Occupation, coming from the French Fascists.

When we learn that in 1941, in the name of the National Council of the Protestant Church, Pastor Boegner expressed his indignation as a Christian at the measures taken against the Jews by the Vichy government, *Le Pilori* wrote: "Incredible, but true ... An inadmissible letter from the head of the Protestant church ... This Christian cannot be unaware of who killed Christ." The article suggests that the pastor, a traitor to the cause of France and a saboteur of Marshal Pétain's work, should share the fate of his "Jewish brothers."

In the meantime, in view of old persecutions, renewed suspicions, and humiliating measures emanating from the Catholic clergy – despite the fact that after Vatican II these measures have tended to disappear – who can say that no trace of resentment remains among French Protestants? Outside France, we would still have to examine the situations in Quebec and Northern Ireland, where the problem of identity and the social question intersect with the religious problems. At least in these two democracies dialogue has finally begun. Even if, as in France, mutual resentment persists.

2

Revolutions: The Role of Resentment

To what extent do revolutions constitute one of the extreme expressions of resentment? That is a question that obviously accompanies the following observation: the transformation of revolt, whether it is aristocratic in 1789 or bourgeois in 1917, into a revolution is said to be something grafted onto the immemorial rebellion of the lower classes. Does the identification of the role of resentment in these events make more intelligible phenomena previously seen as conflicts between orders or classes?

Both in 1789 and in 1905, the protagonists in these revolutions counted for a time on the monarch to put an end to the suffering and the anger that were their origin. But that time did not last. Violence rapidly became generalized and submerged everything else. It was at first a consequence of the disillusionment arising from the monarch's refusal to allow a challenge to absolutism or an upheaval in the social order. Then, this violence expressed a resentment from which emerged the idea that nothing could henceforth hinder a regeneration whose flag had already been run up. We find these traits and the connections linking them in these two revolutions.

France, 1789–1793: against the king, against the aristocrats, against the rich

In 1789 François-Noël Babeuf – later known as Gracchus – wrote to his wife, horrified by the murders of the state councilor Foulon, who had been accused of speculating in grain, de Launay, governor of the Bastille, and de Flesselles, provost of the merchants, on 14 July:

> I understand that the people are taking revenge, and I approve of this revenge when it is satisfied by destroying the guilty, but today could it not be cruel? Tortures of all kinds – drawing and quartering, the wheel, burning at the stake, flogging, hanging, executioners everywhere among us have pursued it in such bad ways ... The masters, instead of making us civilized, have made us barbarous, because they are barbarous themselves. They are reaping and will reap what they have sown, because all that, my poor wife, will have, it seems, its terrible consequences: we are just at the beginning.

For the preceding three or four centuries, the effects of the growth of state control and the violence of the feudal system had intersected, creating a feeling that power was being used arbitrarily against those who were its origin. When in 1789, following the financial crisis and the aristocratic revolt, Louis XVI asked that *Cahiers de doléance* (lists of grievances) be drawn up in preparation for the Estates General, he was to some extent viewed as a redeeming arbiter.

"So the day of wrath has arrived," we read in a pamphlet, *Dies Irae ou les Trois Ordres au jugement dernier*, "the day of justice and revenge. When the king invested by his people mounts the throne of truth to examine everything, found everything, reform everything, regenerate everything ... We shall see the base rapacity of the nobles, the hypocrisy and greed of the priests, and what the people has suffered in the way of humiliations, vexations, and injustices."[3] According to an anonymous Memorandum, the inhabitants of the area around Limoges had been persuaded that the king, wearing wooden clogs and peasants' clothes, had come to the church and entered the pew of a lord who had driven him shamefully away, and that was why the king ordered all his subjects of the Third Estate to burn these pews, and then he was supposed to have ordered the burning of deeds.

---

[3] Quoted by de Baecke, pp. 215–16.

Jean Nicolas observes that the intellectual training of the people who wrote the *Cahiers* – members of the minor nobility, notaries entrusted with public documents, lawyers, vicars, and curés, the latter more or less imbued with Gallicanism or Jansenism, and generally anti-establishment – owed at least as much to their social practice and their environment as it did to the theories of philosophers and economists. They had done their political apprenticeship in the field, and therefore were perfectly well aware of how outdated the old structures were. "Hence they found it easy to espouse the views of the groups consulted, whose grievances intersected with their own resentments."[4]

> People will no longer say, 'If only the king knew, if only the king knew.' The king, the best of kings, the father of a great and good family will know. All vices will be destroyed. Happy and virtuous industry, probity, modesty, honor, virtue, patriotism, gentleness, equality, concord, work, pity, economy – all these great virtues will be honored, and wisdom and goodness will finally reign alone. The mutual affection linking princes and subjects will elevate this throne, the only one worthy of the King of the French.

This *Cahier* from a little commune near Saintes not only announces the "Good News," a world that is about to change, it confirms the expectation that the sovereign can only subscribe to the change, incarnate it and lead it. However, after this call to the nation, so full of hopes, he no longer behaved as the French expected him to. To be sure, he doubled the representation of the Third Estate and let the Estates General transform itself into a Constituent Assembly, but continued the voting by orders – so what good did it do to double the representation of the Third Estate? He conceded and then drew back, drew back and then conceded, so that it seemed that despite a certain good will and despite or perhaps because of his weakness, he ended up joining the party of those who "asked him not to give in to the movement." Later on, by refusing to ratify the civil constitution of the clergy, which many priests had accepted, by trying to retain a right of veto over the bills passed by the assemblies, he aroused the distrust of part of the lower classes in Paris. His flight to

[4] Jean Nicolas, p. 540.

Varennes in June 1791 completed the rupture of the bond of affection that united the monarch and the nation. But all that was, of
course, "the fault of the aristocrats."

In fact, even before these events, the rancor of the masses
against the privileged had been expressed in the *Cahiers* of 1789.
The inhabitants of a village near Cézanne, for instance, demanded
the end of a society divided into orders and equal rights for all.
"We, poor inhabitants, it is we who willingly or not serve the
King and the fatherland. It is we who pay for the cannons, the
rifles, the cost of lodging soldiers without any hope of seeing our
children rise to high military office, the door is closed to them."

The refusal to pay certain taxes and rents did not, of course,
begin with the writing of these *Cahiers*. But the uprising in Paris
spread to some extent, and in the countryside the rumor that an
aristocratic plot was afoot – a false but plausible notion – led to
the "Great Fear." The peasants attacked the chateaus to burn the
documents on which were written the rents that had to be paid
to the lords. This uprising, which came in the wake of half a
century of riots, took place as soon as the abolition of feudal rights
seemed in danger.

The coincidence of the dates shows that the generosity and
clear-sightedness of the liberal aristocrats were produced by this
"Great Fear," which led to the "Night of 4 August" on which
many of the privileges were abolished. This was "an event unparalleled in history, because this decision to break the bond between
feudal property and property as such was irreversible."[5]

However, the hatred of taxes and rents was only one aspect of
the peasants' resentment. They also sought to put an end to the
offenses to their dignity. They already wanted to destroy all the
symbols of the nobles' superiority, also attacking the bourgeois
who were "living nobly." For example, in the region of Bray, many
nobles were prosecuted because they wanted to keep their reserved
pews in church. Numerous pews were therefore burned, along
with the weathervanes of the chateaus destroyed, among other
symbols. After the night of 4 August, the old myth of the world
upside-down had aroused a mad hope, it had been almost magical:
"Madame," wrote the Duchess of Brancas's steward, "the people

[5] François Furet.

is the master, it knows too much. It knows that it is the stronger party."[6]

In addition to the peasantry's grievances against the aristocracy, there were those of the bourgeois who aped the gentry. "The formidable explosion of resentment against the nobility and its way of life at the time of the French Revolution," Max Scheler wrote, "would be completely inexplicable had this nobility not been invaded by the common bourgeoisie, which, on acquiring the nobles' land, had also appropriated their rents ... This new feeling of equality among the arrivistes with regard to the dominant class explains the violence of this resentment." In the Estates General as in the Constituent Assembly, the borderline between nobles and bourgeois crossed over the division into orders, since 58 delegates of the Third Estate belonged to the hereditary nobility (Chambord, Mirabeau, and others). Others had recently been ennobled or were connected with noble families, or with the first order – the clergy – and nonetheless also felt themselves to be the victims of discrimination.

The interest of Max Scheler's judgment is that it emphasizes the gap – small, according to this approach – between the hereditary nobility, on the one hand, and those who had been ennobled and other bourgeois "living nobly" on the other: which aroused in the latter a resentment proportional to the humiliations it had suffered. Madame Roland complains that when she and her mother were invited to dine at the chateau of Fontenay, they were served in the butlery. Barnave acknowledges that he became a revolutionary the day that a noble drove his mother out of the loge she was occupying in the Grenoble theater. Bergasse could not be presented to the king without producing a noble lineage going back to the sixteenth century. The lawyer Mounier speaks of humiliating exclusions that grew during the aristocratic reaction of the 1780s: "all the doors of honor were closed to the Third Estate." Dubois-Crancé, whose father had been ennobled, did not pardon the way courtiers at Versailles had scorned him when he was a musketeer. Pierre-Louis Roederer could not buy an office of *maître de requêtes* because "he lacked sufficient noble lineage." "What a disappointment not to have seen the nobility put in its place,"

---

[6] Ibid., p. 218.

Campmas wrote in the late summer of 1789. "That mob with coats of arms ought to be humiliated," Gallot wrote to his wife.

But the expression of such feelings did not appear suddenly. The upper bourgeoisie did not feel itself to be united with the nobility within a single elite, despite the fact that their fortunes, while not nearly so large, were nonetheless considerable. But the roots of their rancor against the hereditary nobility were not to be found there. These roots were ancient, as Gaultier de Biauzat clearly states: he had always been scandalized by "the iniquities and other humiliating behaviors." If he had never denounced them, it was "out of fear of the blows that were to be expected under the old empire of abuses." He had a family to protect and couldn't challenge "those rich egoists." It was only when the king asked the French to express their feelings that he was able to communicate "his own."

The peasant fury directed against the aristocratic order and the excesses of monarchical power, like the nobility's rancor against the monarch's ingratitude, which surfaced a hundred and fifty years after *la Fronde* – these are phenomena rooted in the distant past. The word "resentment" appears in 1593, in *Le Dialogue du Français et du Savoysien*, associated with the hereditary nobility's annoyance on seeing the bourgeois enter its ranks: "The resentment arising from pain that they (the princes) felt on seeing themselves scorned (by the king) to give luster to the aggrandizement of these newcomers."[7]

Seeing the identity of their group "polluted" aroused resentment, this time among the nobility, against late comers and those responsible for this adulteration. We will encounter this sort of thing again. But a wound of a new nature was about to be opened up among those who were the driving force of the Revolution. It was to re-open other wounds, which did not fail to have effects on the course of events.

In a study of the 1917 revolution, I once drew attention to the specific role of lawyers and jurists at the beginning of Czarism's fall – Kerenski, Nabokov, Godnev, Lenin – which was comparable to that of the first revolutionaries in 1789 – Desmoulins, Le Chapelier, Danton, Robespierre, and others. I pointed out that

[7] R. de Sulinge, quoted in Vaken, p. 145.

their profession predisposed them to have a better acquaintance with the problems people encountered in their everyday lives, and thus to listen to them more than to men of letters or the "Philosophes." They were more capable of giving the revolutionary movement the meaning it had at the outset: putting an end to injustices, to abuses, and to privileges, to attacks on dignity.

Timothy Tackett's work allows us to refine this hypothesis. First, he shows that in 1789 there were few writers or philosophers among those elected. Condorcet, defeated in Paris, had to get himself elected elsewhere, as did Marmontel and others. Bailly speaks of "a great disfavor in the assembly for men of letters and academicians." But still more, Tackett's research shows the preeminence of men of the law, 218 magistrates and other lawyers, which accounts for the juridical flavor that dominates the Constituent Assembly's debates. This also brings out the existence of a kind of social borderline between the lawyers and the bourgeois businessmen and other ennobled persons mentioned earlier. Moreover, an examination of their dowries shows that out of fifty cases in the Third Estate, only two (Armand-Gaston Camus, one of the first presidents of the Constituent National Assembly and the creator of the National Archives, and Mougins de Roquefort) received a nice dowry of forty thousand livres, while those of most of the lawyers and jurists were four or five times less. Among the elected representatives with the most modest incomes – along with those of the clergy, which were even poorer – these lawyers and jurists were by far the most active orators. It was among them that the most vindictive orators were soon to be found. Above all, it is significant that after having attacked "the aristocracy of privileges" they directed their condemnation, like Robespierre and Marat, against "the aristocracy of money." "What will your Constitution be?" Robespierre asked at the Jacobin club. "A true aristocracy, because the aristocracy is the state in which a part of the citizenry is sovereign and the rest are subjects. And what aristocracy? Is it to fall once again under the yoke of the aristocracy of the rich that we have thrown off the yoke of the feudal aristocracy?"

In truth, with the exception of these petty officials, lawyers, and others, the majority of the Third Estate's representatives was composed of well-off people who had already felt humiliated in the Estates General when they had to dress in black while the members of the other two orders appeared in richly colored clothes. They had no immediate connection with the lower classes. Furthermore, in the Estates General as in the assemblies that emerged from it, there were neither artisans, nor small merchants, nor peasants.

It was this Paris working class that had taken the Bastille, brought the king back from Versailles on 5 and 6 October, and stigmatized his flight to Varennes, seen as a sign of his duplicity. Wasn't it treachery to have approached the frontier and those who were soon to become overt enemies of the Revolution? When the nation was at war with a coalition of its neighbors orchestrated by the king's brother-in-law, the conspiracy was clear, whereas the sovereign's tergiversations confirmed his villainy: he resisted the Assembly's decisions when the fatherland was in danger. The threats of invasion thus made the people oppose the monarch. The popular uprising of 10 August 1792 put an end to what Varennes had begun.

But just as much as the fall of the monarchy, this uprising marked the emergence of a new, popular power, the Paris Commune, an offshoot of the municipal authorities where the protestors from the political clubs had prevailed over the original elected representatives. Its clerk, Tallien, noted, "We cannot break the Commune without striking the people," echoing the anathemas declared against the king and the Legislative Assembly by Robespierre, Marat, and Danton. This popular power, henceforth incarnated in Danton, challenged – and this was something new – the Legislative Assembly, which had been elected by the nation, but on the basis of a poll tax, that is, by the wealthy.

It was under this reign that a wave of criminal terror swept over the capital as soon as the people had broken into the Assembly and taken the king from the Tuileries Palace and imprisoned him in the Temple. The symbolic obstacle represented by the monarch had disappeared. Nothing any longer held back the violence that had been contained up to that point. Anger and vengeance targeted the aristocrats and, this time, the refractory priests who rejected the civil constitution of the clergy. To be sure, there had already been acts of violence and crimes, notably during the Great Fear, the rumor of an aristocratic plot that led in July 1789 to pillaging, riots, murders, and arson all over the country. But these had been spontaneous, whereas in September 1792 the massacres appear to have been coordinated by activists connected more or less with the Commune's committee of surveillance. If this committee was fictitious, the activists were genuine killers coming from the crowd and the suburbs. And the Jacobin eulogists, who had in their way sounded the alarm and had become, like Danton, the incarnation of the Commune, watched these horrors with half-closed eyes.

However, in the provinces spontaneous atrocities had already preceded those in Paris. Two priests had been killed in the Orne area on 19 August, another in the Aube, and a bailiff in Lisieux. In Bouches-du-Rhône, the electoral assembly heartily applauded the news of the massacres in Paris. Houses belonging to suppressed religious orders were emptied and put up for sale. The cities then experienced a terror that no longer targeted only fine homes and chateaus, but the rich themselves, as Marat and Robespierre had wished, or those who, given the food shortages, could become rich, the monopolizers. Soon, in Paris and elsewhere, committees of surveillance and other extraordinary tribunals identified, arrested, and sentenced suspects. And the Convention elected in September 1792 soon wanted to take control over society into its own hands. So that terror came from above, from the Convention's Committee of Public Safety and its Committee of General Security, which gradually absorbed the Commune's powers.

From then on, denunciations and suspicions raged, fed by a whole series of resentments, of personal vengeances disguised behind the public Good or Virtue. Camille Desmoulins, who was executed in turn like many other deputies, described this deleterious atmosphere, borrowing from Tacitus:

Does a citizen enjoy a certain popularity? He's a rival of the prince, who could incite a civil war – Suspect.

Does he, on the contrary, flee popularity and keep to himself? This retired way of life makes you noticeable, makes people treat you with respect – Suspect.

Are you rich? There is an imminent danger of the people being corrupted by your generosity – Suspect.

Are you poor? Well, then, we've got to keep an eye on this man. There is nobody so enterprising as someone who has nothing – Suspect.

Thus, the field of action for resentment, envy, and vengeance grew. Everyone might become a privileged person in his neighbor's eyes. But the forms taken by acts of violence, and those who were the victims of these acts, were regularly governed by another motivation that marks a *change* in the course of the Revolution. We discern its appearance in the nature of the speeches given by a young, unknown lawyer, hardly more than an adolescent, Saint-Just, during the king's trial. His attacks were devastating.

The day before, a representative had emphasized that in the absence of a law regarding the status of the monarchy, this trial was impossible. Fauchet explained that executing Louis XVI would provoke pity. Rouzet noted that Louis XVI had appointed ministers who were *philosophes*, convoked an Estates General, and abolished the mainmorte in his domains. Saint-Just replied:

> Of course the king could be judged in accord with the law. But the point was not to hold a trial but to make a political act. The king was not a defendant, but an enemy. The simple fact of reigning makes him guilty. He has fought the people, and he has lost. He is a foreign prisoner of war. You have seen his perfidious designs; he is the murderer of the Bastille, the Champ de Mars, the Tuileries. What enemy, what foreigner has done you more harm?

The interest of this text resides in its novelty: it is situated on a terrain entirely different from that of the orators of 1789. It is no longer a question of putting an end to arbitrary power, of relieving the wretched people, of appealing to equity. It is a political act that will give meaning to the victory and make it possible to go further. It is not a matter of being equitable, but of being efficacious. Of eliminating the obstacles barring the route to the Revolution's advance.

For the Revolution to be able to carry out its work, that is to contribute to the regeneration of society, it is not enough to have destroyed privileges, the object of all resentments; all the symbols and signs of the old feudal system have to be eliminated, and in particular the monuments "raised to prejudices and tyranny." A kind of devastating rage, a vandalism stigmatized by the Abbé Grégoire, was afoot in the country, destroying sacred busts and libraries along with all the other emblems of the past. Cloisters and other religious sites were not spared, their demolition being connected with de-Christianization. Even their orange trees (signs of luxury) were cut down, "because Republicans need apples."

But this past and the inequalities of which people wanted to rid themselves was also embodied in the knowledge of these elites against whom the resentment of those who knew nothing raged. "Men of talent" were its victims: Lavoisier was one of the first, then Condorcet, who, persecuted as a Girondin, committed suicide after having written a hymn to the glory of the Revolution, *L'Esquisse d'un tableau de l'esprit humain* (Sketch for a Historical Picture of the Progress of the Human Mind). Vandalism was thus identified with terror, and still more with Robespierre, who incarnated "barbarism, ignorance." That was a problem, because these barbarians were no longer foreigners, the enemy, aristocrats, but a mob within, the very one that had contributed to the success of the Revolution.

Resentment against the privileged had given way to an avenging fury against anything that was thought to block complete regeneration. Egalitarianism took priority over the aspiration to freedom, to equity. The supporters of democracy challenged every trace of superiority. Resentment against the elites thus became the adulterous child of these different crossings.

"The people who know, they're all rascals," Maxime Gorky said at the time of the Russian Revolution. The body of the elites thus donned a different garb, and since then, it is in part against elites that resentment is expressed, no matter what their origin: birth, money, merit, competence.

Russia, 1917: a complete revolution

In its élan, the revolution of February 1917 was the most complete of all time. However, posterity thinks of the October revolution as the Russian Revolution, because it lasted. And also because it inscribed on history the socialist project, that is a transformation of society in view of the Reason inherited from the Enlightenment. It remains that in its spontaneity the February revolution was the immediate response to aspirations that the peoples of Russia bore within themselves. Was it only the peoples of Russia? We shall see.

In Moscow, workers forced the owners of their factories to learn the fundamentals of a future labor law. In the armies, soldiers

invited their chaplain to attend their meetings, so that they could
give meaning to his life. In the province of Penza, the mujiks asked
their landlord how many children he had, in order to divide up
his land equitably. In Odessa, students told their professor of
history what the program of study should be. Even children made
demands: "for those under fourteen, the right to learn boxing so
they could force the big kids to listen to them." It was the world
turned upside down. It was the outcome of a few memorable
events. When Czar Nicholas II fell, after five days during which
the capital had risen up against autocracy, poverty, and defeats,
and during which soldiers disobeyed their officers in refusing to
fire on protestors, the whole country was shaken by a turmoil
unparalleled in its frenzy and enthusiasm.

Within a few weeks, society rid itself of all its leaders: the
monarch and his jurists, the police, the priests, government officials, and bosses. Every citizen felt free, free to decide at every
moment how he would behave and what his future would be. As
the bards of the revolution had announced, people were entering
into a new era in the history of humanity. An immense cry of
hope rose up from all the Russias. I have myself read through the
thousands of telegrams – never opened – that were received by the
provisional government and the Petrograd soviet during the first
weeks of this revolution. In them are heard the voices of all the
wretched, all the humiliated. They were revealing their sufferings,
their hopes, their dreams. "No, Mr. Kerensky, we can't stand it
any more ..." And, as if in a dream, this society then experienced
a few unforgettable moments.

This upheaval had been preceded by a century and a half of
peasant revolts anticipated by Pugachev's insurrection. A small
land-owner, Pugachev proclaimed himself czar in opposition to
Catherine II and organized a vast peasant rebellion of Cossacks.
A first highpoint was reached with about fifty revolts in 1842.
Despite the liberation of the serfs in 1861 and the subsequent
agrarian reforms, notably those of Stolypin in 1906, the peasantry
remained unsatisfied because only a minority of them had been
able to purchase land, and then only by going deeply into debt.
In 1917, it was no longer making requests, but demands. For
example, "someone explain to us, right now, why the magnates
who have thousands of deciatins of land (a deciatin was equivalent
to a hectare) are exempt from military service and do not defend

the fatherland, whereas we, who have no land, must risk our lives to defend it in an emergency?" The peasants also asked that state lands be seized, and even those of the great landlords, if they were not being cultivated. "When we want to take these lands, it's anarchy. When they take away our sons, it's patriotism." Their anger and resentment then manifested themselves without restraint.

Less virulent, the factory workers complained especially about the humiliations to which they felt they were subjected. Not even a wretched salary: the workers at Ekaterinodar, for example, often received only a ruble and twenty copecks a day, or the equivalent of two four-pound loaves of bread. Especially, they said, there is no medical help at the factory, no washbasins, or if there are, they are unusable; no boiling water or even hot water. "For the loss of sight in both eyes as a result of an accident at work, the indemnity is a hundred rubles." They are asked to pay a series of fines without even knowing why. And they are subjected to a dishonoring search. "All that is inhuman. We Russians are not Tatars."[8]

"When I entered a factory for the first time," Alexandra Kollontaï wrote, "and I saw those poor wretches, all at once I felt that I could not go on living so long as that had not changed." This wound would not heal, she said, until these poor people had another life. Kollontaï was an aristocrat who joined the Bolshevik Party and became one of its leaders.

Prince Piotr Kropotkin's account follows another itinerary. A personal resentment, coupled with an acute awareness of the people's wretchedness, made him the leader of anarchism, the heir of Mikhail Bakunin. He explained clearly how this happened. One of the hundred and fifty servants in his household got drunk and broke a plate. His father had him given a hundred lashes as punishment. The whole family and its servants were dismayed by this tragedy. Little Piotr was then about ten years old; it was 1851.

> I was choking with tears. Immediately after the meal, I ran to find Makar hidden in some corridor and I tried to kiss his hand. But he pushed me away, weeping, and told me, without reproaching me: 'Leave me alone. Do you think you won't be just like that when you grow up?'

[8] Anonymous petition sent to Kerensky by factory workers.

When he was still a child, this first trauma revealed to Kropotkin that he felt closer to his servants than to his father, who was a soldier and a prince, but whom he already despised, or even hated. Since his mother's death, his father had allowed his second wife to erase her memory by removing from the house the furniture and pictures that she had cherished. Whereas his mother had once saved his father from dishonor when he had been accused of mis-appropriating public funds. She had taken the humiliating step of appealing to the official in charge of the case, who happened to be one of their former serfs. Thanks to what she did, Kropotkin's father was able to "put on his red trousers again and another plumage." Had this father spent even a night in a bivouac, or taken part in a single battle? All rigged out, he imposed terror and military discipline on his estate. And Piotr, like his elder brother, was as afraid of his father as the serfs on his estate were. "The true love that I have known came from them," Kropotkin writes in his *Notes*. We discern here his resentment (he uses the word) against his father, his family, the army – and the established order. Having read Marx and the other socialists, especially Saint-Simon and Proudhon, Kropotkin said to himself: "I shall take a different path." But after these wounds suffered in childhood and adolescence, how many prisons and exiles were still to lead him along the path of anarchism!

About thirty years later, in 1887, another young man, Vladimir Iyich Ulyanov, also declared, "We will follow a different path." He too had changed character as the result of a trauma: the execution of his idol, his elder brother, hanged for his terrorist activity. He was leaving school when he learned of his brother's arrest. He ran to tell his mother, who had been widowed shortly before, and who left for St Petersburg to beg that her son be pardoned. But in vain. When Vladimir, then seventeen, read in the St Petersburg newspapers that his brother had been executed, he threw them to the ground, trampled on them, and exclaimed: "They will pay for this!" "Who's 'they'?" a neighbor lady asked. "I know who they are, and that's enough," Vladimir replied.

What he meant could be glimpsed. At the time of the famine of 1892, five years later, he was studying for his law degree and had joined a Marxist group in Samara. He explained that

> Famines result from a certain social order and only the abolition of that order will be able to prevent them from returning. The

Prod DB © Mezhrapbom Russ/D.R.

The son's resentment against Czarism, which has not kept its promise.

current famine, which was inevitable, contributes to future progress by pushing the peasants to move to the cities. Thus a proletariat is forming that will lose its faith in the Czar and precipitate the victory of the revolution. The so-called society's desire to come to the aid of the starving is easily explained, because this society is part of a bourgeois order that feels itself threatened with disturbances and even with total destruction. In reality, all this babble about helping the hungry is no more than a manifestation of the unctuous sentimentality that characterizes our leading societies.

At this time Lenin, as a Marxist, rejected terrorist attacks such as those in which his brother had participated: he approached political problems "differently." Up to that point, in fact, he was one of those revolutionaries who thought that to change the social order, it would suffice to eliminate the Imperial family or "to crush the imperialists with the same ferocity they employ against us." The rallying cry was "Kill them all, in the cities, in the villages, in the hamlets. The revolutionary party that will take power must ensure its dictatorship by whatever means ... We must exclude any reactionary element from the assembly – supposing there are still any of them alive."[9] This exasperation, this extremism were also the expression of a certain impotence.

In his history of Russia, Klyuchevsky, who is a sort of Macaulay or Carlyle of that country, wrote that since the death of Peter the Great in 1725, what characterized Russian society, from the peasants to the notables, was that no one thought "any change could modify the traditions of this country."[10] That meant that the idea of reform, even if it had powerful support, was something incongruous, and that apart from making serfdom more or less severe, any idea of change seemed inconceivable. One sign of this belief identified by Alain Besançon is the frequency of dreams in Russian novels, which is revelatory of the society and its desires. Hidden desires that these dreams express, in Pushkin, Dostoevsky, Oblomov, and Chernyshevsky, for whom revolution will fulfill or will come to fulfill the dream. Unless it turns into a nightmare.

But the important point is that the feeling of powerlessness appears in all its forms during the nineteenth century. You will be like your father, the mujik, who does not believe his condition will improve, tells Kropotkin. Confronted by the ineffectiveness of the reformers or revolutionaries, people tell each other "We'll have to do things otherwise." And this change can only be dreamed about. Everything suggests that the trauma of the victims, the former serfs, will one day explode, as the slave revolt exploded in ancient Rome. After the abolition of serfdom, and given that famines were occurring, the Marxists, including Lenin, called for an accelerated transition to the industrial era. In this way a powerful working class would emerge and achieve the revolution. This transition took place slowly, but it did take place.

What Lenin wrote about the famines reveals the way he approached problems: in this we see in miniature, as it were, the approach of a doctrinaire man, a doctrinaire Marxist in this case. In the famines he saw first of all an opportunity to advance the revolutionary project, and proceeded to analyze its causes, explaining them sociologically. We see here as well the denial that the class enemy has any generosity or pity, and in Lenin himself an absolute indifference to the sufferings of the wretched. Thus, in

---

[9] Common watchword of the "terrorists" before the triumph of Marxism.
[10] Vol. 5, p. 231.

Lenin, Marxist reasoning regarding the failure of past experiences intersected with a particular resentment.

To the personal trauma felt by a certain number of revolutionaries – as in the cases of Kropotkin, Lenin, or Kollontaï – we might add that of many others who were also wounded, humiliated to have been excluded from secondary school or the university for ideological or religious reasons, Jews in particular. We can observe in them the same kind of intersection between personal resentment and doctrinaire reasoning: Leonid Martov, for example, a Jewish Social-Democrat, thinks that pogroms have something positive about them, as the first sign of peasants' participation in political action, even if it was against Jews! To the annoyance of the workers, peasants, and minorities, and to the impatience of the revolutionaries, must be added the irritation of all the members of the intelligentsia who felt themselves excluded from the management of the country.

During the February revolution, Grand Duke Cyril set an example by joining the Petrograd soviet, followed by the Cossacks of the Guard in his Majesty's regiment. Few remained steadfastly faithful to Nicholas II: Count Keller, Count Zamoyski, and the former minister, Bark, who was offered a ministry but refused it "as a matter of principle." No one tried to save Czarism. When the "missionaries of the revolution," Guchkov and Shulgin, declared at the Petrograd railway station that Nicholas II, who had abdicated, was to be succeeded by Mikhail II, they were almost lynched. "Down with the Romanovs, Nicholas, Mikhail, it's all the same: the white radish is as good as the black radish, down with the aristocracy." Protected by the agents of the provisional government, the missionaries were able to escape.

But there was hardly any resentment against the person of the Czar. Nothing like what Louis XVI experienced after the flight to Varennes. And few demands were made regarding him. Out of a hundred workers' motions addressed to Kerensky and the provisional government, only two asked for "measures" against the Czar; in addition, three others came from peasants, and four from soldiers, for a total of nine out of more than three thousand telegrams and motions sent from all the Russias. However, after the events in July, there was grumbling. For fear of an act of violence – or that the monarchists would try to kidnap him – Kerensky had the Czar and his family transferred to Tobolsk, where they would be safe. Then in October, they were moved to Ekaterinenburg, on the orders of Sverdlov, who, with Lenin and Trotsky, had been one of the organizers of the October insurrection. But already at the time of the civil war there were increasing demands that the ex-Czar be put to death, or at least that he be put on trial, and there was discussion about entrusting Trotsky with this matter. But with the advance of the "White" troops, the Bolsheviks, fearing that they would liberate Nicholas II, took it upon themselves to execute him. Russia was informed of the execution by a simple press release, and remained wholly indifferent. At that point, while the lower classes had often been more radical than the Bolsheviks, the latter still did not really control the press. Neither the Reds nor the Whites applauded, protested, or reacted to the announcement. There was neither compassion nor resentment.

An invisible turnaround, the passage from a revolution that, in the name of equity, intends to put an end to arbitrary power, to a revolution that, in order to survive, takes revenge for past outrages – that is a phenomenon that we see in France in 1792 and find again in the Russia of 1917. During the first two months of the revolution of 1917, the resentment of the lower classes had been contained; it had been expressed only imperfectly, through a few violent explosions, especially in the armies, and in the countryside, where many land-owners' homes had been burned. But participation in revolutionary action had in a way neutralized, converted, channeled this resentment.

In March 1917, when the abdication of Nicholas II was announced, the country's people were filled with delight. "It's over, now it's over," exclaims a militant in the crowd who is weeping tears of joy. Then a hand taps his shoulder from behind. It's an old woman, who tells him: "You're mistaken, little father. It's not over, not enough blood has been shed yet ..." The revolution is going to change directions.

In June 1917, when the first congress of the soviets assembled, a large portion of the hopes aroused in February still persisted. To be sure, violent acts had been committed in the countryside and in the armies, but relatively few, so real was the feeling of a victory of equity and fraternity. A happiness that recalled that of February 1848 in France.

Kerensky and certain members of the provisional government had a great deal to do with this; as minister of justice, Kerensky had facilitated the escape of the designated victims of popular resentment: policemen, former ministers, and others. He had asked the wealthy to donate their jewels to relieve the suffering of the most impoverished. These gestures had made him instantly popular, even if many revolutionary militants considered them ridiculous.

In June, annoyance began to be expressed because the "bourgeois-socialist" coalition government tried to be "conciliatory" by waiting for a constituent assembly to decide the future of the society. Holding that assembly when the war was not yet over and the soldiers could not participate in the election was considered anti-democratic by the majority of the elected members of the soviets. For their part, the Bolsheviks thought, with Bukharin, that if the revolution did not put an end to the war, the war would end up smothering the revolution. And in fact, that is exactly what happened: in the name of national defense, and in view of the Allies' refusal to consider the peace agreement without annexations or reparations proposed by the Petrograd soviet, what survived of the old order sought to regain the upper hand. In the armies, which were preparing for an offensive, the high command required a return to military discipline; in the armament factories, the eight-hour day had still not been introduced. It was then that Lenin announced at this congress of the soviets that his party, which had only 105 elected representatives out of about 1,200, was prepared to take power. This statement was met with loud laughter, a sign that the majority of the representatives considered themselves democrats. Kerensky then reminded Lenin of the fate of the extremists in France in 1792, and later on, in Russia in 1905.

Lenin replied that once in power, he was prepared to "arrest a hundred capitalists," which triggered another burst of laughter: so that was what Marxism was? But that was not what was important. Confronted by the revolution's inability to move forward, Lenin resorted to extreme, surgical measures. They were claimed to be necessary. No resentment was involved: Lenin did not want to arrest capitalists because they had behaved in an inhuman way, which would have been in accord with the logic of the revolution against the injustice and inhumanity of the former masters; for him, this measure was not rooted in moral principles, in respect for human dignity. No! Like Saint-Just, Lenin adopted the point of view of a war that is waged against one's enemies – in this case, of class war; he wanted to prevent the mechanics of the revolution, its advance, from grinding to a halt, and this imperative had priority over any other consideration.

Just as the nature of this change had gone unnoticed in 1793, the one that Lenin was initiating was not fully appreciated either. But for someone who remembered the lesson drawn from the help given to victims of the famine, there was a continuity in his way of approaching problems, which was, in these two situations, independent of his personal resentment. Lenin was reasoning like a doctrinaire and a strategist. Thus, in October, he correctly gauged the changed power relationship between a government that no longer had any power, given the multitude of committees and soviets that exercised it at the base, and this headless state constituted by the soviets as a whole. Their Bolshevization resulting from the bankruptcy of the provisional government, the military offensive having failed, and with disorder on the rise, Lenin thought he could launch an insurrection, now that General Kornilov's attempted putsch to re-establish order had failed.

Just as in France in 1792 and in the spring of 1794, it was the resistance to the victors of October that freed up the repressed energy of those who had been expecting the revolution to provide vengeance or regeneration. This resistance could be assumed by the political rivals of the new power, that is, the non-Bolshevik revolutionaries who had been excluded from the management of affairs, or else, explicitly and clearly, by "bourgeois" organizations or the bards of counter-revolution.

But the mujiks and the businessmen who, like their predecessors in 1794, held back part of their products in order to evade requisitions did not see themselves as enemies of the government. Alongside the effects of the civil war that was beginning with the Whites, their "resistance" to the government of the soviets unleashed the worst of terrors, with its attendant horrors. "We need a Fouquier-Tinville," Lenin told Bonch-Bruyevich, one of the promoters of the Red Guard, in 1917. "It would put down all this counter-revolutionary rabble ... a solid, proletarian Jacobin. That would be Felix Dzerzhinsky, because he has spent more time in Czarist jails and knows what he's doing." "Terror is going to take very violent forms, as it did during the French Revolution," Trotsky added. "A bullet in the head, that's what speculators will get!" Lenin said.

"What is the good of a Justice commissariat?" Lenin was asked by Steinberg, a left-wing revolutionary socialist, "you might as well call it "the people's commissariat for social extermination!" "Excellent idea," Lenin replied, "unfortunately we can't give it that name." "Shoot the revolutionary socialists, deport them!" he said to the communists in Yelets. "Unfortunately, I can't give you written authorization to do it."

"It is life that dictates the Cheka's path," Dzerzhinsky explained at a time when this madness was afoot only in a few cities. His remark fully contradicts, moreover, the dogma of the Marxists, notably that of the Bolsheviks, who condemned the spontaneity of the massacres. Henceforth, it is the opposite, and so we find Lenin stigmatizing Zinoviev, who is worried about this uncontrolled violence that the Cheka wants to rein in – yes, the Cheka: "I strongly protest," Lenin writes to Zinoviev. "We are compromising ourselves: whereas in our resolutions we don't hesitate to strike mass terror into the representatives in the soviets when it is a matter of acting, we brake the entirely founded initiative of the masses. That is not possible. The terrorists will see us as wet blankets. We have to encourage the energy and the mass nature of terror."[11]

Thus, to imagine that the violence of late 1917 and 1918 emanated from the Bolsheviks alone or from the encouragement they gave to "this life that dictates its path" would be to Bolshevize history. But despite the fact that since their victory in October, they had incarnated a revolutionary majority, they could not delegitimize themselves by admitting that popular resentment and anger was more than they could handle.

Later on, having increased their ranks with all the little apparatchiks who came from the committees of popular government, they would indeed be the agents, the sole agents, of the Red Terror. In fact, the similarities between what happened in France in 1792–1793 and what happened in Russia go further. In addition to the use of the same terms – "enemy of the people," "sabotage," "monopolist," "purge society" – the atrocities committed in 1917–1918, like the violence committed against officers between

[11] 26 June 1918.

July and October 1917, owe more to Bolshevik propaganda than to their own initiative – just as the massacres of September 1792 owed more to the speeches in the Paris Commune than to their own initiative. And the Convention took this terror into its own hands, just as the Bolshevik Party was to do. Except that both of them "politicized" this violence. In both cases, resentment was instrumentalized.

In Russia, this violence coming from below attacked everything that represented or incarnated the old order: officers, government officials, and notables of all kinds, men and women "with white hands," in Ukraine and everywhere else.

Thus, gradually, in the committees and other soviets, the old managers of the society, driven away or exterminated, made room for elements coming from popular milieus, who were soon called "apparatchiks," a phenomenon that I have called the "plebianization of the state apparatus." Bolshevik power depended on these apparatchiks to the extent that they became part of it.

"Before, you were the masters, now it's our turn," a soldier told his captain. He felt he was taking his revenge after centuries of repression and servitude.

Resentment against the elites

In France, during the revolution, resentment against the privileged gave way to an egalitarian madness. Any trace of superiority, even a symbolic one, was suspect and challenged. It is true that the denigration of the elites, whatever their nature, had preceded the Revolution: it had to be shown that this elite was immoral. Like Marie-Antoinette, who was supposed to be surrounded by libertines, and whom lampoons accused of all sorts of depravity. Or like the monarch and his aristocrats, who were caricatured as impotent. Later on, even before the Terror, when there began to be a threat of food shortages, Marat denounced "Danton's indecent little suppers," while there was much gossip about the scandalous behavior of the rich. More than that: scientists (Lavoisier, Condorcet), whose knowledge was inaccessible and perpetuated the past, were also executed.

In its turn, imperial Russia had its own gossip. I have seen the little notebook that records Rasputin's "performances" before court ladies whose husbands were later promoted to high offices.

And the news circulated. But the surge of purity that was incarnated by the early Russian Revolution broke with these forms of denigration. Moreover, revolutionary militants never ceased to repeat that the iniquities of the past were not attributable to the acts of individuals, but to institutions – which were going to be changed. In March 1917, with a view to preventing an explosion of resentment, Kerensky, who was then the minister of justice in the first revolutionary government, proposed the abolition of capital punishment. Violent resentment nonetheless spilled out of the most generous or most extreme speeches. And the elites, including those of the cultural world, and no matter how much they had supported the poor and helpless, became victims.

Russia: from premonition to resentment

If most of the members of the intelligentsia and artists (except for Gorky and Lunakarsky, the future people's commissar for education) did not participate in the revolutionary events, which they thought did not concern them personally, a whole "literary civilization" had nonetheless been engaged in a political battle against autocracy. With Leo Tolstoy, it had supported the workers and unfortunate mujiks whose condition had scarcely improved, despite the reforms carried out by Alexander II and then by Stolypin. Above all, this cultivated society, well described by Chekhov, had lost faith in its own future – like Masha, the disappointed lover in *The Seagull*, always dressed in black because she was mourning her own existence. Sad, desperate, Russians were grieving for their own history.

Nothing really changed in the country, except in the world of business. This had to do with the state, whose chief principle was resistance to change. In 1894, Nicholas II had called "a mad dream" the notion that Russians might participate, through some kind of constitution, in the government of their own country.

Bulgakov, who was soon to publish *The Master and Margarita*, noted that the Russian intelligentsia challenged everything: the political system, religion, marriage. The populists and Marxists called for socialism; Bonch-Bruyevich justified atheism; while Alexandra Kollontaï legitimized free love. An immense chasm separated them from the czar, his ceremonials, and his popes.

Nicholas II even asked whether the word "intelligentsia" couldn't be removed from the dictionary.

"Successful or not, the revolution will be just as absolute as the autocracy," said Merezhkovsky, a disciple of Dostoevsky. And Konstantin Balmont, the poet, added:

> Our czar, feeble-minded and blind,
> Prison and whip, who shoots and hangs,
> The hour of punishment awaits you ...

"Let the storm break," demanded Gorky, the beggars' bard. When the storm did break the first time, in 1905, Rosanov-Varvarin wrote in *Rousskoïe Slovo*: "After having seen the admirable spectacle of the revolution, cultivated people wanted to collect their fine fur coats from the cloakroom and go home to their comfortable homes. But their furs had disappeared and their houses were in flames."

After war broke out in 1914, pointless massacres, shortages, and anger increased, and the intelligentsia, like the members of the Duma who were close to them, proved incapable of channeling and containing a new revolution that was born spontaneously but whose hymn they recognized because they had written the words to it.

The intelligentsia's frustration was followed by a premonition of catastrophe: "The age of humanism is over," wrote Biely, a poet of the real, "now comes that of holy barbarism ... There will be a leap over history." The revolution did not arise from a revolt, the workers attacking the industrialists or the peasants their landlords, but from the fact that the old government had not been able to defend Russia. Indeed!

According to Biely, it was henceforth "the revolutionary individual who was afoot ... the masses becoming the executive apparatus of these sportsmen of the revolution." He saw that the time when well-structured organizations were directing the revolutionary movement was over. From then on, it was going to be the reign of uncontrollable individuals manipulating the crowds.

"Culture is a head full of holes from which everything leaks out." That was a feeling widely shared, even by Gorky, who, taken to the Petrograd soviet on March 1 – by Sukhanov, who was one of its founders – so that he could be applauded, declared there, ill-humoredly, that first of all a commission to protect historical monuments had to be created. On the first day of the revolution in February, were they already in 1793, when busts and libraries were destroyed?

When the czar fell, an immense cry of delight had risen from the capital. The regime had collapsed as much as it had been brought down. And the more people had benefited from the czar's favor – grand dukes, generals – the more they rushed to support the new regime. The poets were not the last to rally to the regime: Blok, Mayakovsky, Essenin, Korolenko. They proclaimed that "Now all is possible ..." Everything was possible? In fact. For example, it was possible that the great stars of the theatre and the opera, previously acclaimed, were now immediately rejected, booed, even forced to emigrate – though they had thought they would be popular forever and had defended the good cause. We can imagine their resentment.

For instance, Chaliapin in 1905 had signed, along with Rachmaninoff and Rimsky-Korsakov, a petition against the arbitrary rule and absence of freedom that reigned in the country, in particular in the theatre, where the production of a play by Gorky had been prohibited. Although Rimsky-Korsakov was automatically dismissed from his position at the Conservatory, demonstrations took place in the theatres, notably the state theatres, where censorship was the most vigilant and which were a favorite site for spontaneous political demonstrations. The spirit of the time was revealed, high society in the orchestra and the loges, the less well-off students in the cheap seats and standing room. At the end of a performance in which he had been wildly applauded, someone in the stalls asked Chaliapin to sing *Dubinskaja*, the song of the deported. He did so, an affront in the presence of the empress. But another time ...

The chorus of the Bolshoi opera in Moscow intended to present a petition to the czar. It was decided that after the first scene of *Boris Godunov* the curtain would come up to reveal the whole chorus in a supplicant pose directed toward the empress's loge while the petition was read. When the curtain was raised, in accord with the desired effect, Chaliapin, who was not in on the plan, and who was singing the part of Boris, thus found himself there, in front of the petitioners, dignified, a colossal personification of imperial authority in his superb gold-trimmed costume, the Monomakh's crown on his head. In that moving moment, Boris stood facing Nicholas II ... Then, instinctively, Chaliapin knelt down and joined the petitioners, to the great anger of part of the audience: he should have remained standing, facing Nicholas II, as if to defy him. He was never pardoned for this. Other artists who had kept their fans saw that in a period of revolution people had little desire to go to the theater, because the show was in the streets – where in parades and processions, much creativity was displayed.

But even if they had wanted to go to the theater, it had been taken over by collectives that had sometimes changed the repertory or simply substituted themselves for the troupe that was already there. That meant that a very great freedom, not to say a certain anarchy, prevailed in the country.

However, in the throes of the civil war that was beginning, writers and artists discovered with alarm that the desire to control cultural activities started to manifest itself. For example, in Petrograd as in Saratov or other cities, *Proletkult* (proletarian culture) appeared. This was a proletarian cultural institution that presented itself as the fourth force in the worker's movement, along with the Party, the trade union, and the cooperative movement. What was this institution that thus emerged from the earth?

Few writers or artists except for those who had been active in revolutionary milieus knew about the socialist movement's cultural project. Speaking in the name of the working class, asserting that it would be the agent of social revolution – that posed all sorts of problems, and had been frequently debated since the revolution of 1905.

Criticizing the revolutionaries, Makhaysky, himself a Marxist, wrote shortly after the revolution of 1905: "Waiting for workers, who are doomed to a lack of culture by their wretched living conditions, to become capable of directing production and organizing social life amounts to guaranteeing the exploiters a parasitical life for eternity." He added: "These revolutionaries tell the worker: 'You want to be as educated and cultivated as I am, so instruct yourself and study instead of getting drunk.' Criticizing these leaders, Makhaysky concluded: "You want to be rich? Well then, work and save."

We see that this argument presupposes that there is only one culture, one body of knowledge, and that these are moreover identical with each other and will be the culture of the elites. At that time, of course, no one denied that there might be several cultures, for instance folklore or the cultures of foreign peoples. That there might also exist a back-and-forth movement and crossings between the different cultural heritages and the official culture, called "bourgeois," which includes and supplants them – in short, which exercises a hegemony: that was also an observation that was made, but it was not central; at least not in revolutionary milieus. The dominant idea turned instead around a new pole, which might be "socialist culture," whose status and nature remained, however, to be defined.

However, the very principle of this project was challenged, and an alternative to it was proposed. Two paths could be taken. On the first, the working classes could "acculturate themselves" through social and economic conquests. Thanks, essentially, to education – a project that the socialist "schools" for the working class began to implement, with their "good" authors, from Zola to Gorky. Then the conditions for a genuine democratization of political life would be gradually established.

Or else – the second path – this project is deemed a mystification and the only true revolution will be the one that expropriates the owners of material goods and the holders of cultural goods, intellectuals and other educated people who have arrogated to themselves, thanks to those riches, the right to tell others what to do by becoming party members, managers, and so on. In a certain way, the socialists – especially the German socialists, but also the Russian and French socialists from Kautsky to Lenin – followed the first path until the Second World War, and even after it. The victory in October and the establishment of Communist parties strengthened this choice and then extended it to the whole world.

Early in the twentieth century, the second path was followed by Bogdanov, and later by Mao Zedong, at least during certain parts of his career, and by some utopians in 1968. Its eulogists set out to destroy established values and knowledge and to substitute for them the culture that the working classes, in emancipating themselves, would reconstitute on the basis of heritages that they have had to repress. Those who followed this path tended to adopt an anti-constitutional, often anti-academic attitude. They wanted to put an end to the resentment of popular groups that still had an inferiority complex with regard to educated people, by opposing the latter's knowledge, which they defined as outdated and reactionary, a new culture. This group did not define proletarian culture "by popular arts and traditions, by folklore, although it was related to them; it has nothing to do with teaching the masses to read and write, without rejecting it," Jutta Scherrer explains. Proletarian culture has to be a creation.

With regard to its ideal of proletarian revolution, its project of a society "without contradictions," *Proletkult* holds that "there is no place for diversity." In addition, intellectuals are not to have access to it. It is not a matter of denying their heritage, but of organizing culture in a different way. "We do not ask you," *Zizn'Iskusstva* (Cultural Life) explains, addressing, among others, filmmakers, "to make films that will be understood thirty years from now, but films that will educate the masses today." It is the members of the avant-garde, "the cultural nihilists," who are the target here. "What they do, I don't understand it at all," Lenin said. To be sure, *Proletkult*'s attempt to strengthen its organization collided with the hegemonic will of the Bolshevik Party. At the ministry of culture, Lunakarsky had to decide what cultural operations the state would subsidize. And in every city, the various collectives – the former theatres, the *Proletkult*, literary groups – competed for subsidies, to the despair of writers and artists. So that for the intelligentsia, not only did the fall of the autocracy not correspond to its expectations, but it nourished its resentment against a government that betrayed its hopes. The object of this resentment was no longer autocracy, the czar, but Lenin and Bolshevism. "The intelligentsia hates our guts," Lunakarsky wrote to his wife. "The officials' boycott is impeding our work."

If officials were the only problem! In the army, the officers who had rallied to the new government were suspect; in the offices, the statisticians were suspect; in the hospitals, the doctors, like Zhivago, were suspect; in the factories, the engineers were suspect. But the government needed these managers, these specialists, the *spets*, as they were called. While keeping a sharp eye on the *spets*, the Bolshevik government – particularly Lenin and Trotsky, who were moved by a certain technocratic spirit that was concerned with efficiency – wanted these managers, these intellectuals, to serve the regime.

The people's power, which the Bolsheviks' political practice had managed to graft onto the state apparatus, intended to keep an eye on everything that emanated from the elites. Intellectuals already found it impossible not to participate in *Proletkult*, and upper-level technicians could no longer enroll in trade unions. For when he was a victim, the czar's subject was his subject in every way; to oppress him, there was no need to share power. Once the revolution had occurred, the citizen naturally requisitioned the totality of powers. And he excluded those who were suspect, to the point that the masses soon no longer had confidence in these leaders, even the revolutionaries, even the Bolsheviks, though it spared them. It saw them as bourgeois, like the *spets* – and they were in fact bourgeois, with the exception of Shlyapnikoff, the sole worker in the leadership of the Bolshevik Party.

Those long lines of deportees being sent to the Solovki Islands in the far north, filmed by Goldovskaya in 1922, and who were well-clothed and worked hard, were they *spets*, dissenting revolutionaries, or avant-garde artists, all of them former eulogists of progress?

France, May 1968: a reply?

Far from the capital, a student strike broke out because a request for funds had been turned down. Most of the professors had refused to participate in the strike because "they did not get involved in politics." That is precisely what their students reproached them for. The students thought that "the point of studying was to enter into life, studying was not an end in itself." The university was supposed to be open to understanding society, not close itself to it. But while the students were debating these problems and agitation was going on in the city, the professors were preoccupied with a very different issue: the election of the rector.

However, the students undertook to critique the teaching imposed on them, they changed the history curriculum, and changed the grading system. At the same time, in the capital the actors and staff had taken over certain theatres, assuming the manager's role to modify the repertory. However, these events did not occur in France in May 1968, as one might think, but in the spring of 1917, at the University of Odessa and in the theatres of Petrograd and Saratov. Striking concordances, but for France in 1968, and despite *those facts*, they were in no way a repetition of

1917, because the latter had been erased by the soviet, Communist, Trotskyist vulgate. They nonetheless prefigured what happened in France half a century later, because the people behind the events in France claimed they were following the example of the Russian revolution. Are not the events of 1968, particularly in France, in their own way, and to a certain extent, the expression of a kind of resentment against the elites? To be sure, at first, and rightly, they were seen as a youth movement that drew others along in its wake. It initiated a social dynamics that transformed the student revolt into a political crisis. Therein consisted one of the differences with the student movement in the United States, which had led to the birth of a kind of cultural counter-society, with its hippies, or, in Germany and in Japan, to a political counter-society, with its "Red Army." In all these situations, the revolt was nonetheless associated with the postwar baby boom, which resulted in the simultaneous arrival of a great many individuals on the labor market. This served as a detonator for a malaise that had preceded these young people's entry into life.

At the university, and even in secondary school, young people had begun to question the way society functioned, they had become politicized. In 1967, in Strasbourg, a brochure published by the Situationist International denounced the status "of a stratum that is being massified and whose future can only be to carry out a subversion of institutions." What lent a certain scope to their frustration, namely that they would not be able to play a role in society that corresponded to their aptitudes, also had to do with the fact that advertising had given this age group a collective identity as new consumers. In addition, cinema, and even more, music, had acted as educators, a sort of center of energy that freed the body and constituted a counter-culture. Rock 'n' roll was the agent of this revolution, which celebrated the end of the age of restrictions – that of the family, school, work – and the escape provided by deafening amplifiers. Between the nonviolence of the hippies in the United States and the violence of the "rockers" (*blousons noirs*) in French cities, there was one common trait: the challenge to their parents.

The hippies reproached their parents for thinking of nothing but producing and consuming, and thus being constantly in contradiction with the moral principles they pretended to take as their basis. "Since you're bombing children in Vietnam and reciting the

Bible, we'll be dirty, but we'll have "clean souls," these young American pacifists said.

As for the French rockers, who were the children of factory workers, they reproached adults for not having been able to transform society, although they constantly protested its abuses. Perched on their motorcycles, with heavy chains draped across their chests, these *blousons noirs* – my students at the Lycée Rodin – told me: "You see, sir, we're sick of our dads' stupid little strikes – all that just to get a raise of a hundred francs, 2 percent ... Everything has to be destroyed for things to change."

Relations between fathers and sons have probably always been marked by ambiguity. Kafka was not the last one to observe that they expressed mutual resentment. "I am well aware," he wrote to his father, "that your childhood was very hard, and that you had to push a cart barefoot through the snow to earn a living. And I also know that it is true, how could I deny it, that today I have a far more comfortable life. But why should I feel grateful to you for that?" Except that in 1968 young people's politicized action presented itself as such, and their protest was not a simple challenge or reproduction of their parents' grievances, as were those of the young Communists, Christians, or other groups. Not only did they live in a parallel culture, but they had their own morality, a specific vision of society that the American cinema expressed in two cult films, László Benedek's *The Wild One* and Nicholas Ray's *Rebel Without a Cause*, which made Marlon Brando and James Dean famous. In France, the New Wave films – notably those of Chabrol, Truffaut, and Godard – revealed what was left unsaid in social relationships and constituted a parallel culture. When, in February 1968, Henri Langlois, the archivist of these films at the Cinémathèque, was dismissed, a huge crowd consisting mainly of young people protested vigorously. A few months later, they also demonstrated against the war the United States was waging in Vietnam and against the repression being carried out by the soviets in Prague. The traditional political dividing lines had collapsed. But deference towards all leaders, whether in politics or the trade unions, and towards the elites had also collapsed. The principle of authority was questioned, defied in the university and in families. "Why do we need professors?" young people asked even before television became a parallel school ... Seeing how the intellectual elites – Raymond Aron as well as Roland Barthes – found themselves overwhelmed by a movement whose meaning they did not grasp, we understand that certain of their students now thought them sterile and that "they should hand over their positions to young people who have something to say."

In this context, the democratization of teaching seemed to be an illusion, since the selection of students excluded most of those who were not the best at the time of the competition, that is, those who were handicapped by the absence of a cultural heritage, according to Pierre Bourdieu and Jean-Claude Passeron. This mode of recruitment became suspect when it provided an anchorage for the meritocracy. This observation showed that the great principles defended by politicians and professors were in fact an illusion refuted by the facts. These young people had encountered professors who continued to repeat programs of study conceived for another time, for a minority, without having themselves critically examined the content, meaning, or utility of their teaching or its usefulness. To some of these young people these professors appeared to be the holders of a capital, or oppressors of a particular kind, monopolizing knowledge as if it were merchandise.

Egalitarian demands reached the point of parody. At the University of Vincennes, for example, a philosophy professor gravely wondered if he was being equitable, because there was only one rostrum in the auditorium, and he was the one using it. At the University of Chicoutimi (Quebec), during a general assembly of professors, students, and administrators, the representative of the students' collective gave an "unprecedented" speech: "This university being the least favored by the state, the worst teachers are sent here. But they get the same salary as the professors in Montreal. Whereas students' costs are higher than elsewhere, because of the distance: we demand that part of the teachers' salaries be allocated to the students." The motion was approved and sent to the administration, which promised to consider it.

It was in this context that a kind of resentment was able to develop, no doubt fed by other frustrations. In its shadow developed a so-called "pedagogical" movement. Its declared goal? To regenerate teaching methods and stimulate the student's own activity so that he would control the progress of his knowledge. Behind these intentions there was also, latent and proceeding from below, the idea of depriving the elites of their eminence, the desire to carry out a kind of cultural revolution in which those without diplomas or with poor ones would constitute the infantry. This resembled what was done in 1917 in the name of *Proletkult*, which had challenged the foundations of "bourgeois" culture and was also the expression of a certain resentment against the elites.

In the world of letters, linguistics was the instrument of this operation that dismantled great texts in the name of a "scientific" formalism. In history, it used the Annales School as a pretext for doing away with narrative and chronology, which were a priori ideologically suspect. For them, it substituted formatted questions and answers, which were, moreover, very distant from the problematization established as a method by the historians Marc Bloch and Lucien Febvre. A new group of teachers thus emerged, more interested in pedagogy than in culture.

An "anti-aristocratic" movement driven by a rather similar kind of resentment arose in the theatre. In 1968, the Odéon theatre was invaded by actors and stagehands who had not been chosen by Jean-Louis Barrault and his troupe. Barrault himself was insulted and expelled from his theatre without knowing why, as often happens when resentment explodes. The protestors also criticized the nature of the repertory proposed by the great figures in the theatre – as happened again forty years later in Avignon, where the festival of the established troupes was upset by those whom the organizers had not chosen for the most prestigious evening performances. This chain of resentments connected various social groups that were, naturally, not necessarily moved by the same anger – no one died – but by a desire for revenge. Unless some of them also wanted to regenerate society.

Today, such manifestations of resentment against cultural and other elites are accompanied by new features arising from the globalization of the economy and the development of telecommunications. Robert J. Schiller, an economist at Yale University, notes that this resentment pits transcontinental businessmen with multiple networks around the world against those whose competence is rooted in their rural area or city, and who, though they do not know the world, know their fellow citizens. Their ways of life increasingly separate the elites that proclaim their local rootedness from the "international" ones for whom the nationality or origin of their interlocutors matters little.

In his own way Jean-Jacques Rousseau had anticipated this phenomenon two centuries ago, at a time when the idea of Europe inherited from the Enlightenment was spreading. He wrote:

> Europeans who are no longer Englishmen, Frenchmen, or Spaniards [...]. What does it matter to them which master they obey, to which state's laws they conform? Provided that they find money to steal and women to seduce, they are at home everywhere.

A "counter-revolutionary" revolution: Germany

For Germany in 1918, as for France in 1940, defeat was a trauma. Its ultimate consequences were the Nazis' seizure of power in Germany and the immediate establishment of the Vichy regime in France. These were true counter-revolutionary, or conservative, revolutions, no matter how they have been described, which does not mean that they were similar in the eyes of those promoting them. However, we should not associate these revolutions exclusively with the two defeats; or, indeed, confine the history of Nazism to the period 1918–1945 or that of Vichy to the period 1940–1944. If defeat served as a lever allowing the establishment of these two regimes, their origin is far older: it is, moreover, common to a large part of Central and Eastern Europe, and accounts for the depth of German resentment after 1919 and French resentment after 1940.

During the half-century preceding World War I, European society underwent unprecedented changes. To the recognized, declared authorities of the past – the priest, the monarch, the law, the officer, the boss – were now added new, anonymous and uncontrollable masters: prices on the world market. It was the markets that suddenly lowered agricultural prices, bringing about the ruin of the rural areas; it was they that triggered an economic crisis, determined fashions and opinions. In this strange world that transforms itself so quickly, age-old activities disappeared, trades were born and died in the course of a single generation, one patented invention displaced another and died in its turn. And always in the name of progress, law, and freedom.

These changes have thrown individuals into an atomized society. People have been uprooted, eliciting a feeling of abandonment. In the countries most affected by this exacerbated development of capitalism, the need to find recourses, help, solidarities, constituted a form of resistance to this liberalism seen as the source of all evils. Trade unions and corporations developed or reconstituted themselves in conjunction with mass political parties. "People are tasting the instinctive pleasure of being part of a herd," Maurice Barrès wrote in his *Cahiers*.

This was true in France and in Germany, where this modernity was opposed by the churches (because these changes were accompanied by a secularization of life), the anti-capitalists of the revolutionary left who were counting on the working class to establish socialism, and those who clung nostalgically to the past. In France, after the defeat of 1870, the fear of demographic and economic decline was endemic. Crises that revealed a serious malaise exploded, whether in the Dreyfus Affair or the Panama scandal. In Germany, widespread discontent proceeded not only from external economic conditions – the omnipresent straitjacket of British power that impeded expansion – or from the fear of war. It proceeded from a general dissatisfaction that seeped up from the abrupt changes the society was undergoing throughout its culture. It was precisely at that point, during the years before 1914, that Nietzsche and Scheler wrote about resentment in society. Scheler spoke out against the bourgeoisie and its values, liberalism and "the Jews that incarnate it," parliamentary government – "a bourgeois joke," Lenin called it, and man's exploitation of man. This resentment arouses aspirations that are contradictory but all passionately experienced, whether it is a matter of nationalism or internationalism. The project of a socialist revolution, or that of a conservative, nationalist reaction, thus drew Germany and France into the same malaise resulting from the shock of an excessively abrupt economic change. And in Germany, on the fear of not being able to expand because it lacked enough colonies; and in France on the fear of disappearing as a great power.

Even before there were large organizations associated with the "left" and the "right," we see that some people were able to move from one side to the other. Georges Sorel is emblematic of this; he is described as the father of both revolutionary syndicalism and fascism. Just before the First World War, that was also true of the internationalist socialists and pacifists, whose leaders, at the Stuttgart Congress or elsewhere, did not group themselves by socialist tendencies (revisionists, radicals) but by nationalities, thus reproducing the order set up by the governments they claimed to be combatting by resisting the war. The French socialists were revanchist with regard to German socialists and amicably condescending with regard to the Russians, who had few socialists in the Duma. So that all these internationalists acted in accord with the existing modes of relationship between states and belonging to a country.

It was this national feeling that swept away everything in 1914; it was, Benedetto Croce said, an "instinct deeper than socialism and all its arguments"; it "gives roots those to those who find themselves uprooted." "I don't need abstract truths," said Paul de Lagarde, one of the prophets of German anti-Semitism and the desperate advocate of a regeneration of his country, which he considered destined for a luminous future, for it is "a model of civilization," as Thomas Mann also wrote in 1914.

When war broke out in 1914, the earlier vows of pacifism were forgotten at the first trumpet blast, in Germany as in France. Beyond the Rhine, "a growing excitement due to the feeling of insecurity"[12] was manifested. First of all, people said, the war was going to transform life, and then victory would settle everything. That is the German myth that preceded the French myth, in 1918, of the *der des ders*, the last of wars.

Returning home after three or four years spent in enemy territory, German soldiers who had "come back unvanquished from the battlefield," their own soil inviolate, enthusiastically participated in ceremonies that crystallized their illusions. Suddenly, Germans discovered the clauses of the armistice, and then, in the Versailles Treaty, the victors judged their country guilty and responsible for the war. The violence of the resentment against those who accepted such clauses is equalled only by that they fed among the so-called victors. The war was over, but in people's heads it wasn't finished. As for the civilian population, whereas during the war life had gone on as before – except for increasingly severe restrictions as the war dragged on – the Spartacist revolution of 1918 produced abrupt changes in everyday life: strikes, shootings, parades, broken windows. Whereas during the war the meaning of events was clear, those the civilian population was now witnessing appeared incoherent and confused.

[12] Jeismann, p. 262.

The humiliation of being treated as guilty when one had not felt the weight of defeat and considered oneself the bearer of a superior civilization (German eminence in the domain of the sciences, technology, and philosophical and musical culture was widely recognized): all that added to the resentment – operating, according to Thomas Mann, as an "internal Versailles" – against those who accepted this situation. Soon signatories of the Versailles Treaty – Matthias Erzberger – were assassinated by the extreme right, as were some revolutionaries who thought that Germany had a share in the responsibility for the outbreak of war – Kurt Eisner – and those who thought paying reparations would make it possible to restore a peaceful climate – Walter Rathenau. During the very first years after the armistice, there were 376 political assassinations, 354 of which killed leftists. With the occupation of the Ruhr and inflation – the mark/dollar exchange rate rose from 10,425 to one to 4.2 billion to one – we see, in 1923, the first Hitlerian surge, with a failed putsch sponsored by General Ludendorff. It was above all the – unprecedented – inflation that threw the middle classes into deepest despair, reviving hundredfold the feelings of insecurity that had appeared ten years earlier, on the eve of the war.

The obligatory deliveries of coal as reparations aroused protests that expressed the anger of a humiliated society whose desire for vengeance was growing – but was powerless. That is what made it generate projects for recovering its grandeur and a glorious future. In 1922, Moeller van den Bruck, the theoretician of neo-conservatism, was already calling upon German youth and urging population growth that would allow the strength of German genius to spread its wings: they had to "take advantage of the apparent defeat in order to prepare for true victory." This hope was popularized by Oswald Spengler, who referred to the "disciplined solidarity inherited from Prussia, which alone can protect the white race against the assault of the inferior classes." That other revolution, which was to overthrow the Weimar Republic established in "the foreigner's railway cars" and install a Third Reich called for by Moeller van den Bruck, could only be national. That is why a galaxy of journalists discredited representative and parliamentary democracy and outlined what this country, relieved of its political parties that were fighting among themselves, and that was threatened by another "coup" by the

Communists, ought to be. Hitler took up all these ideas and gal-
vanized them in *Mein Kampf*, which refers, with Goebbels and
Alfred Rosenberg, to the nature of the battle that Aryans must
wage against the European Internationals and their agents inside
and outside the country, the Jews.

This is the form, analyzed by Philippe Burrin, that resentment
took among these leaders, whom the crisis of 1929, a veritable
social apocalypse with its six million unemployed and thousands
of bankruptcies, was going to confirm in their opinions. Nazism
responded to it with a plebeian, counter-revolutionary social revolution, as well as with measures of vengeance against those whom
the Führer considered responsible for these disasters. Three months
after he had taken power, five hundred thousand persons (Communists, Social Democrats, Liberals, and Christians) were sent to
forced labor camps thought up by Göring. The Jews were to
follow them. Victory was supposed to resolve all Germany's
problems.

It was indeed personal resentment that initially drove Joseph
Goebbels's animosity toward Jews. He had just taken a doctorate,
written a Christian tragedy, *Judas Iscariot*, and tried to get a job
as editor of the *Berliner Tageblatt*, a newspaper run by a Jew who
supported the Weimar regime. His articles were returned to him.
Another humiliation: a collection of political notes, *Michaël, A
German Destiny*, was rejected by a publisher, Franz Ullstein, also
a Jew. This double wound transformed him into a violent anti-
Semite quite unlike the man who had once dedicated a poem by
Heine, a Jew whose works he was to burn fifteen years later, to
Hanka, his first love.

This personal resentment was soon grafted onto the anti-
Semitism of Karl Kaufmann, the head of the National Socialist
party in Elberfeld, to whom he offered his help and who introduced him to Hitler. Kaufmann, a veteran of the *Freikorps*, had
belonged to the pan-Germanist and anti-Semitic group *Shutz-
und-Trutzband* (Offensive and Defensive League), which was
responsible for Rathenau's assassination.

Contrary to what he implied, and as Brigitte Hamann has
demonstrated, nothing shows that Hitler was an anti-Semite
before the 1918 armistice, though he was certainly a xenophobe
in Vienna, where he fulminated against the presence of Czechs,
Slovenes – and Jews, too, though on the same basis as the others.

Nothing during the war, his correspondence, for instance, indicates an identifiable anti-Semitism. So that unlike Goebbels, he was not moved by any personal resentment. We know, for example, that no Jew was on the committee that eliminated him on the entrance examination for the Vienna Academy of Fine Arts, and that he even had a certain affection for his mother's physician, who was Jewish. It was later on, in Munich, that his anti-Semitism crystallized, though that "purely German" city dear to him became one of the centers of the 1918 revolution: the head of the council of workers, soldiers, and peasants was a Jew who was an independent Social Democrat, that is, who was close to the Spartacists.

Hitler also observes that the Hungarian communist Bela Kun was a Jew, like Karl Marx, and like those whom he called "Judeo-Bolsheviks" – Trotsky, Zinoviev, and others – to use his term, who might pervert German identity as they perverted Russian civilization. Thus he was primarily fighting the Jew as a revolutionary, and he soon wrote, with Dietrich Eckart, a little work called *Bolshevism, from Moses to Lenin*. The second aspect of his anti-Semitism is the attack on Judaism, which he considered to blame for having given birth to Christianity, which de-virilized the Nordic races, as Hans F. Günther, one of the most popular theoreticians of "Nordicism" taught. Racism ties together these different considerations, inspired in Hitler by Wagner's spellbinding art and the writings of Gobineau and Houston Chamberlain, and of Nietzsche as well, though Hitler had not read him. Moreover, Hitler misinterprets the concept of the superman – an internal battle – and he did not see that Nietzsche condemned and despised anti-Semites. Whereas in Goebbels's case the anti-capitalist dimension of his anti-Semitism is central, it was just as much the battle against the "international Jewish conspiracy" that mobilized Hitler. While his anti-capitalism was the heir of the anti-bourgeois climate before the war, his antipathy to the "Jewish conspiracy" was given new life by the German translation of the *Protocols of the Elders of Zion*, that entirely fabricated fraud that describes the tenets of an imaginary plot. Kellog has recently shown that it was recent White Russian emigrés from the Baltic countries and the Ukraine who brought the *Protocols* with them in their suitcases and helped give a synthetic shape to the anti-Semitism of the German extreme right.

These different registers are not taken up in the same way. Thus, in Hitler's private conversations, in particular the ones recorded by Martin Bormann, or again in what Goebbels tells us about them, the hatred of Jews is above all a hatred of the people who gave birth to Christianity – "its priests' turn will come later," he repeated. But he never made such remarks in public in order to avoid alienating believers.

For Goebbels, Jews were an obstacle to Germany's regeneration – that is, to the regime's success: the German people thus became the Jews' victim, and he insults and threatens them. As an obstacle to the purity of the race – that is Hitler's and Goebbels's constant refrain – the Jew is constantly stigmatized. Later on, when the period of the German–Soviet Pact was over and the first setbacks in the Russian campaign had occurred, the Judeo-Bolshevik conspiracy returned with full force, and Jews were henceforth denounced as embodying the "unnatural" alliance of capitalism and Communism, the two enemies of the German people.

Thus, in the middle of the war, the conspiracy myth and the Aryan myth were joined: the machinery of extermination was already in operation, and the power of resentment ended up taking priority over the German nation's survival: "above all, continue with the extermination," Hitler ordered at the time of the defeat. This was not a written order, but, like the earlier injunctions, it was obeyed. Each of these registers – anti-judaism, the Jews' responsibility for the rise of revolutions, their economic role, the "Zionist" international, racism – had aroused the Nazi leaders' resentment against Jews. The main idea expressed in Veit Harlan's 1941 film *Jud Süß*, made in collaboration with Goebbels in order to popularize it, is closely linked to the racist argument: Jews should remain in the ghetto, they incarnate the lower strata of humanity; if they leave the ghetto and modernize themselves, they pollute the rest of society, and one has to be wary of them. Keeping the Jews at bay, eliminating them, executing them, becomes a matter of public safety. Here we find the three phases in the Nazis' behavior: before the war, they wanted to drive the Jews away in one way or another; then, at the beginning of the war, they confined the Jews to isolated areas, ghettos, in order finally to exterminate them, and when defeat loomed on the horizon, they made genocide a priority, "my only true victory," Hitler said, before he committed suicide. If we know that Germans were moved by a deep resentment against the Versailles Treaty, and that this resentment perpetuated, with unbridled violence, the grievances that Germans nourished before the war, seeing themselves as victims of history, we also know that a certain anti-Semitism already existed in the country, as it did in a large part of Europe.

It remains, however, that neither the extermination of the Slavic populations – which was also part of the Nazi program – nor the total elimination of the Jews had ever before been considered by leaders or groups, no matter who they were. The Nazis made the persecution and then liquidation of the Jews a priority, which it was not for most Germans, even if they were associated with it, and more broadly than they later wanted to admit. If they were able to pretend not to notice, that is because up to the victories of the summer of 1941, they had lived through some unforgettable events. It seemed that since 1933, the mystery of economic mechanisms had been plumbed and the fear of declining in social status overcome, while the authoritarian regime was forgotten because of a war that made everyone equal and sure of the victory of their race. When defeat came, Germans did not express repentance, but they also felt no resentment against their beloved Führer. Thus, it is still a mystery how this civilized society, no doubt the most cultivated in Europe, was able, more or less, to participate in crimes that had never occurred before.

Vichy: to each his own resentment

In France, the resentment expressed immediately after the defeat in 1940 did not flow from an explosion of anger, as it did in Germany in 1919, but from a depression elicited by this disaster unprecedented in the country's history. The other surge of resentment, at the time of the Liberation, took the form of a purgation with vengeful aspects that was also a reaction to the humiliation of defeat and the policy of collaboration. In the meantime, one after another, scores were settled at the summit of the French state, while the occupying power looked on. To each his own resentment.

In 1940, persuaded that the war was over, and that "England will have her neck wrung like a chicken," the new leaders adjusted to the defeat. Switching alliances – "like Napoleon at Tilsit," Pétain said: that is what would allow the saving of what could be saved: the empire, the fleet, and sovereignty over part of the nation's territory. The government's residence in Vichy was seen as temporary.

For Pétain, a new era in history was beginning, that of the "regeneration" of France. "It's because we gave up the effort that we have arrived here," he said, and according to him, the Popular Front was to blame. Blum was doubly guilty for the defeat because he had incarnated that dishonored regime and because he had been belligerent when everyone knew that the war would be lost. But Paul Reynaud and Mandel were equally guilty, because they had urged stubborn resistance to Hitler and then stigmatized the incompetence of the military command, which had demoralized the nation. Pétain also reproached Reynaud for having made Weygand commander of the armies after Gamelin had been dismissed. "I don't like Weygand," he told Reynaud. An old jealousy and an old personal resentment against the man who was adjutant to Marshal Foch, the generalissimo who succeeded him in 1918 and "stole" the honor of the victory from him by halting the hostilities just as, with General Pershing, he was about to enter Germany. Foch's intransigence toward the Germans, after the armistice, of which he had been one of the strongest supporters, paralyzed the policy of collaboration Pétain intended to pursue. Foch ended up getting rid of Pétain when he condemned the concessions made to the Germans: bases in Syria and eased access to North Africa.

Pétain felt the same humiliation, nourished the same resentment toward Laval, who had nonetheless done him the favor of relieving him of the burden of the parliament on 10 July 1940, after seeing to it that the Republic committed suicide and establishing the French state of which Pétain was to be the head. Knowing that he had the support of the great majority of the French people – in January 1940, and thus before the defeat, his nomination to Paul Reynaud's government had been acclaimed by both the left and the right – Pétain was jealous of his authority and he joined his other ministers in reprimanding Laval, who was taking over relations with the Germans and was preparing the meeting with Hitler that Pétain so much desired, but which he and Baudoin, his minister of foreign affairs, had not been able to arrange.

After the meeting with Hitler at Montoire in October 1940, which put the final seal on the policy of collaboration, Pétain got rid of Laval and replaced him with Darlan. But the Germans saw

Laval's dismissal as an affront, and in 1942 Pétain was forced to bring him back as prime minister. In fact, Laval's dismissal in December 1940 helped construct the myth of the Marshal's "double dealing," with Laval appearing as the incarnation of the policy of collaboration, which was confirmed when in 1942 he gave a speech in which he declared that he "desired the victory of Germany." On the other hand, Pétain, making a point of his good relations with the United States ambassador, seemed to be keeping two irons in the fire. If it is true that he liked the Americans and detested the Germans, the latter's battle against Bolshevik Russia and the occupying force's pressure lent strength to the policy of collaboration: the disagreement with Laval and the Marshal's resentment were chiefly personal.

Before satisfying his rancor toward Pétain, old accounts to settle had made Laval the ally and sponsor of the Marshal's policies. Thus, in July 1940, in Vichy, "he had tried to chastise the parliament for having forced him to resign in 1936, and not having listened to him since."[13] He thought that in 1935–1936 only his policy of "small steps" with regard to Italy, the USSR, and England might have made it possible to neutralize Hitler, but the concessions made to the Duce in Ethiopia had caused his downfall. And since Laval, with Briand, had urged Franco-German reconciliation, he wanted revenge on the "warmongers" (*va-t-en-guerre*). In 1938, he had been a supporter of the Munich accords, but a very discreet one, because he detested Daladier, who had signed the accords, and he kept quiet. He also nourished a strong resentment against Great Britain, which had given the Poles its guarantee and thus drawn France into the war, whereas the Poles had taken advantage of the Munich crisis to annex Teschen, and should therefore no longer have expected a Franco-British guarantee. His rancor and his Anglophobia could only confirm him in his policy of collaboration, even if he was opposed to the reversal of alliances leading to a war with Great Britain, which the collaborationists Déat and Doriot were demanding.

In Vichy, Laval resented especially the Marshal's entourage, more or less all of whose members were connected with *Action française* and eulogists of the national revolution blessed by the Catholic Church; they were anti-parliamentarians to the core, if

13 Fred Kupferman.

not anti-republicans, like Alibert and Weygand. This was the age of the national revolution – although its motto, "Work, Family, Fatherland" was thought up by Laval, Pétain having added "Order," and then withdrawn his suggestion – driven by hostility to republican traditions of democracy and representative parliamentarianism that went back to the period before 1914. Even if Pétain had kept his distance from this movement, which could be described as "fascisizing" – and that is why he had been called a "republican marshal" – it remains that many of the ministers and counsellors around him had been involved in the failed coup d'état on 6 February 1934: Scapini, who became "the prisoners' ambassador," Xavier Vallat, the incarnation of parliamentary anti-Semitism, Philippe Henriot, the only speaker as gifted as the speakers of "Ici-Londres, les Français parlent aux Français," Adrien Marquet, one of the founders, with Marcel Déat, of the neo-socialist party, which soon became para-fascist. They were all dreaming only of revenge, and encouraged by the upper clergy, they satisfied their resentment against the Republic, which they regarded as radical, radical-socialist, and socialist, and began by putting an end to the life of the parliament. That suited the Marshal, "who does not talk to those people," whereas Laval, a parliamentarian to the core, had only wanted to settle his accounts with the representatives elected in 1936.

This form of the Vichy regime allowed those who had taken part in the coup d'état attempted in 1934 and all those who, in the period before war broke out in 1914, denounced the people responsible for French decadence, to satisfy their resentment of the "warmongers," the freemasons, and the Jews, not to mention the Communists, who had been ostracized by Daladier ever since the time of the German–soviet Pact.

Stunned by the defeat and by the occupation of more than half the country, during these first troubled years the French were relatively little concerned by the political changes. While awaiting the return of the prisoners, often looking for work, and soon worried about the problems of finding enough food, given the German requisitions, they reprimanded those responsible for the defeat, and more the politicians than the military leaders. But the choice of sides – London or Berlin – was not their primary preoccupation. As Pierre Laborie rightly reminds us, a majority of the French wept over the defeat and at the same time wanted the armistice, and they were able to applaud Marshal Pétain with fervor while rejecting the Vichy regime and being hostile to the occupying power, without for all that being part of the Resistance. For a long time, the majority of the French adapted to the Occupation while at the same time dreaming of liberation.

As for the steps taken against the Jews, until they began in 1942 to take the form of arrests, internment, and deportations, women and children included, it was as if no one, or almost no one, knew what was going on. Had they known, they wouldn't have been more moved, because in 1940 the number of outcasts was large: members of parliament, freemasons, dismissed or deposed public officials, prefects and sub-prefects, even Spanish republicans; what prevailed was silence and indifference. However, Laborie notes, after the autumn of 1942, "the violent feelings elicited by what was happening to the Jews changed the view people had of them." They were henceforth seen, especially women and children, as innocent victims. But what was the importance of this change? "We have to wonder [...] about the meaning of the new silence that prevailed after the Liberation, this time about the genocide"[14] that no one imagined.

By the end of 1942, the situation had changed. The Allied landing in North Africa, the Germans' occupation of the free zone, the sabotage of the French fleet at Toulon, the establishment of the STO (Service du travail obligatoire), young people's refusal to participate in it and the birth of Resistance groups – these were all new events that created a climate of civil war as soon as Darnand's *milice* (collaborationist militia) began to cooperate with the occupying forces to repress, deport, arrest, and shoot those who refused.

The other driving element was the hardening of the German authorities, who were supported by French fascists like Doriot and Déat, who no doubt did not say they were fascists, but were, nonetheless. They reproached Vichy for not declaring war on the Anglo-Americans and broadcast from Paris a collaborationist discourse that, while sparing the Marshal, accused Laval of betraying collaboration and social revolution; on 24 September 1943, a headline in the French fascist newspaper *Je suis partout* read "Laval, cet enjuivé" ("Laval, that quasi-Jew"). That is not what

[14] Pierre Laborie, p. 160.

the German leaders thought; they preferred the ambiguity of Laval's policies to an integration of Vichy France into the Nazi universe. Whence the resentment of the partisans to an adjustment of French institutions and practices to the Nazi model, who saw their hopes dashed. Right to the last moment, their exile to Sigmaringen before the liberation of Paris, Hitler rejected the constitution of a Déat-Doriot government, even though Pétain, who had been kidnapped by the Germans, and Laval had ceased even a fictitious exercise of their functions.

Doriot and Déat were indeed rivals in collaborationism. Still the former came from the Communist Party; a supporter of a Popular Front before there was one, he had been excluded from the Party for having had that idea too soon and, out of rancor, he never ceased to combat it. But if he had a popular base in Saint-Denis, he was prudent. For in 1939, the signing of the German–soviet Pact left him speechless, as it did most Communists. Marcel Déat's itinerary was different. He wrote well, and contributed to *L'Oeuvre*, since he lacked a working-class base; he experienced nothing but disappointments between 1930 and 1945. If he had to be defined, we could say that in France, he incarnates the "man of resentment":[15] humiliated, vindictive, always coming up with new plans for the future. His itinerary shows us the nature and the reasons of the French fascists. He had not wanted France to fight "for Danzig," and in 1940, thinking that history had proven him right, he proposed a whole program for integrating France into a German Europe. He thought that in this way the social revolution he longed for could finally be achieved.

Comparing the situation of France and Germany in the autumn of 1918 and in the autumn of 1940, and developing an argument to justify the creation of a single party in France, Marcel Déat explained that he intended to build a party "copied on the Nazi Party, but which will resemble it as a black Mass resembles a white Mass." In fact, he explains, whereas the Nazi Party was founded on the rejection of the Versailles diktat, the one he planned would be founded on the unconditional acceptance of defeat. While the Nazi Party was founded on the myth of the innocence of Germany,

---

[15] [Translator's note: The French title of Max Scheler's *Ressentiment im Aufbau der Moralen* is *L'homme du ressentiment*. *Ressentiment* is a term widely used in later discussions of the subject.]

which was supposed not have provoked the First World War, the French party was supposed to be based on the myth of the unilateral responsibility of France and England in 1939. Finally, whereas the Nazi Party was founded on the demand for *Lebensraum*, the French party would be cemented by "the French being resigned to becoming a small agricultural state, the orchard and the Luna Park of Hitlery."

These reasons, given just after the defeat, were largely disseminated under the Occupation and had little success, even if they received a rather broad response: the *Rassemblement national populaire* party never had more than 20,000 to 30,000 members in both zones. In 1940, Pétain had rejected the principle of such a party, because "by definition a fraction cannot be a whole," but he had accepted the idea of a supporting force that suited him: it would be the *Légion française des combattants*. On the condition that he be its head. Considering that such a Legion would not advocate Franco-German collaboration with sufficient fervor, and excluded from its leadership, Déat left it, concluding that he had been "tricked"! A glance backward allows us to see that this was not his first disappointment.

A socialist since 1919, anti-clerical and violently anti-Bolshevik, Déat saw the revolutionary left since the split between the Communists and the Socialists in Tours as "a dispersed church being persecuted." For all that the extremists had overestimated the extent to which the country had been shaken by the First World War, and that the Communist Party had "broken the strength of the working class," he considered himself a reformer and believed that victory was to be found in the center, as people said at that time, that is, with the help of the lower middle class. Therefore it was necessary to take part in governments led by the Radical Party. Blum refused to do this, thus proving himself to be, according to Déat, "that nurse of the old party who, instead of awakening it, keeps it in a state of lethargy and sterilizes its renascent strength."

However, Blum had praised this always vigilant swashbuckler, but he did not follow his advice when in early 1929 Daladier, a radical socialist, proposed that he join his government. For Déat, this was not a tactical question. He thought the party should not focus solely on the working class, or remain paralyzed by the threat and the competition of the Communists. The party had to move forward, he explained in *Perspectives socialistes*, a work rather close to the "planist" ideas of Henri de Man. "It was a battering ram that shook everything up," he wrote in his *Memoirs*, where he gives his boastfulness free rein. No one said anything to him: "Total silence in the party, not the slightest review in *Le Populaire*. Neither Auriol nor Blum ever said a word to me about it; unless it was to tell me they'd received it … My break with Léon Blum dates from this book; he finally understood that I was not inclined to behave like a docile disciple and that I would soon become a problem for him … Because my popularity was growing, and a man like Blum, who was born to be a head priest, could not pardon that."

Challenging the distinction Blum had made, even before 1936, between taking power and exercising power, he thought Blum would not permit structural reforms, but only distributive reforms. Thus Déat cast himself as the theoretician of a neo-socialism that split off with Renaudel, Monzie, Marquet, and others, all of them critics of the "trembling talkers" and one of whose slogans, "order, authority, nation" frightened Léon Blum. The goal was to establish forces intermediary between capitalism and socialism, the fascist path constituting, according to them, a possible one for establishing socialism on the condition that freedom and the parliamentary system were maintained.

Hostile to intervention in Spain, favorable to negotiations with Hitler, for "one would have to be a clown to be indignant that Hitler wants to roll back the Slavs," Déat approved the Munich Accords and followed Georges Bonnet, the minister of foreign affairs, who was, out of anti-Communism, prepared to make any concession to Nazi Germany. His article "Faut-il mourir pour Dantzig?" ("Do we have to die for Danzig?"), published in *L'Oeuvre*, made him the leader of the pacifists, the gap between pacifists and bellicists superimposing itself on that between the left and the right. Fearing defeat more than he hoped for it – a distinction that targeted Maurras and his followers, those conservatives that he had always hated, Déat decided, in June 1940, that he was right again, which is very typical of him.

On 5 July 1940, he recommended, in *Le Moniteur*, a newspaper in the provincial town of Puy-de-Dôme, the creation of a *Rassemblement national populaire*, which would be a single party that Bergery and the "neos" (socialists) would join, along with

Doriot and his PPF party, which was overtly fascist. Déat was counting on Laval, but the latter did not include him in his government. Sniping at Vichy, whose collaboration was niggardly, both before and after Pétain's meeting with Hitler at Montoire, he gave Pétain and Raphaël Alibert – a follower of Maurras, a "legal wimp full of rancor," and the author of the law on the status of Jews – the impression that he was working for Laval. He was arrested on 13 December. Then, like Laval, he was released, thanks to the German ambassador in Paris, Otto Abetz, whose favor he enjoyed, and Hitler's express command. "We won't let France be assassinated and we are prepared to do whatever it takes," he wrote in *L'Oeuvre* on 3 March 1941. Henceforth he attacked Darlan and proposed that the government return to Paris, the true capital: "Let's close down Vichy!" But when Pétain made up his mind to bring Laval back, the latter left Déat out of his government again, thinking him not very dangerous in view of Doriot's competition with him.

Déat had regained his footing after the German attack on the USSR in June 1941, but the Germans did not envisage a Doriot–Déat government: they preferred the Pétain–Laval couple. When the *Légion française contre le bolchevisme* was set up "to avoid being denounced as duplicitous and cowardly, it was decided that (like Doriot) we would join the LVF,[16] at least Deloncle, Fontenoy, and I [...], I would take command of the third battalion." But on the day of the Legion's first review, an attempt was made to assassinate Déat, who was accompanied by Laval. Déat had declared that he would never set foot in Vichy, and if he became a minister, he would not swear an oath to Pétain, whom he thought too chilly towards Nazi Germany. The Germans finally forced Pierre Laval to include Déat in his government as minister of Labor and National Solidarity: his appointment was announced in the *Völkischer Beobachter*, the Nazi Party organ, and Laval had to accept his appointment, which Pétain refused to sign.

An "illegal" minister named by the Germans, Déat appropriated one governmental power after another. Laval entrusted the *Service du travail obligatoire* to him, which was no favor. Déat

---

[16] The LVF (Légion des volontaires français contre le bolchévisme), was a French collaborationist infantry regiment created by the Germans in 1941 for service on the Eastern Front.

not only took it on, but found it suited him perfectly. Like other collaborators, Déat was at Sigmaringen.[17] Pétain and Laval having resigned, Déat thought his time had finally arrived. But Ribbentrop advised Hitler to choose Doriot – though Hitler did not take his advice. While he was on his way to meet his rival, Déat learned that he had just been killed by machine gun fire from an Allied airplane. Later, while hiding in the Italian Alps, Déat wrote in his *Memoirs* that history had not proved him wrong.

This pacifist, who had not wanted to fight for Danzig, finally joined the LVF, and though he had been a convinced anti-clerical, he died in a convent near Turin, where he had taken refuge under an assumed name.

If the French fascists had a resentment they could not express, it was the one they had against the Führer. Before 1939, they had all been pacifists, and wanted to believe that a "comprehensive approach" to Hitler's policies might make possible an entente, an expansion of Greater Germany in the east, and even an assault on Bolshevism. But they could not imagine that the Führer wanted not so much concessions as war, as Ribbentrop told Ciano in August 1939, because that was how "the German race would guarantee its incontestable pre-eminence." In the recent past, the Führer had thought his great success had not been the *Anschluß*, which was ineluctable, or even Munich, where he had had to negotiate, but rather the occupation of Prague, a strong-arm act against an execrated nation that its allies, France and Great Britain, had been forced to accept.

Naturally, these French pacifists considered the governments of Poland, France, Great Britain, and the USSR responsible for the war's outbreak. But they were stunned, as they had been by the German–soviet Pact, and refused to see in this anything other than a maneuver on Stalin's part. The French pacifists were unable to express their resentment against Hitler a second time, because from 1940 to 1945 they had constantly wanted their country to be integrated into the Nazi order. More collaborationists than collaborators, they accused Laval of impeding the German-style social revolution they desired so that the Fascist order would prevail in Europe. Once, twice, three times, they even accused

[17] [Translator's note: this was the city in Germany where the Vichy government and other collaborators took refuge in 1944.]

Abetz of sabotage, considering him more German than Nazi; they had in mind the Comintern model of a (Fascist) International with parties that obeyed the "Center." They were unable to see that the Führer did not want to create a National Socialist Europe in the form of a federation of nations, but simply to impose the supremacy of *Deutschtum* and the superiority of the German race.

The *épuration*, that surge of vengeance that appeared when Liberation came, left 10,000 victims, and not 150,000, as the newly freed press suggested in the autumn of 1944. On the other hand, the latter figure is close to that of the number of actual political deportees, to which must be added the 90,000 French and foreign Jews who never came back. But the striking feature is obviously the contrast between the din of the *épuration*, its arbitrariness and excess – since freedom of the press had been restored – and the silence about the German policy of *Nacht und Nebel*, which deported anyone who resisted the Occupation.

It remains that resentment was expressed, as we know, especially against intellectuals like Brasillach, who demanded that "all the Communist representatives be shot, along with Paul Reynaud and Georges Mandel," and who in 1941 asked impatiently: "What are we waiting for?" Or against the announcers on Radio-Paris and other journalists who were also writing in hate sheets like *Je suis partout* and *Le Pilori*, which were subsidized by the Germans but sold well. A vaguer resentment was directed against those, especially in cinema, who enjoyed their hour of glory in German Paris, like Clouzot.

But the real violence, the summary executions, were those that were committed where Darnand's militias, in coordination with the Germans, had tracked down the Resistance, for instance on the Glières plateau. During a few weeks in August and September 1944, when the Wehrmacht was retreating to the North – committing the well-known atrocities, among others those in Tulle and Oradour – fury raged against those who had collaborated with it or betrayed patriots to the authorities.

In Pamiers, for example, which was liberated by the *Francs-tireurs partisans* (an anti-fascist Resistance force) on 18 August 1944, 162 arrests were made in the first five days after the Germans left. An improvised popular tribunal executed twenty-six of those arrested, and the number executed rose to forty-two by the end of August. Thus there was a flood of hatred, vindictiveness, and revenge: "justified executions," in the view of one witness. Another witness told an FFI officer that "he would never have believed that such atrocities were possible in France."[18]

One of the most odious forms taken by this resentment in France was that directed towards women who had had love affairs with Germans. Their heads were shaved in public, because they incarnated the twofold defeat of Frenchmen, whom they had rejected in favor of the occupiers. Conversely, no opprobrium was directed against French prisoners who had done the same thing with German women in Germany – was that considered a form of revenge? Often, it was the fear people had felt for several years that transformed, through resentment, people like you and me into ferocious beasts. Resentment has no homeland.

[18] Pierre Laborie.

3

National Memory as a Way of Preserving Resentment

When, after the defeat of France by Prussia in 1870, Jules Ferry told Clemenceau how happy he was about the annexation of Annam and Tunisia, the latter said: "I've lost two children – Alsace and Lorraine – and you offer me two servants." The pejorative aspect of this comparison, which is scornful with regard to the colonized peoples and unworthy of the nation of the Rights of Man, has been duly observed. But have we sufficiently recognized what was new about identifying two provinces with one's children? Never before, in the age of dynastic wars, had the losses and the gains been seen as inherently traumatic: under Louis XIV and Louis XV, Savoy was traded for Milan, and Lorraine for the Netherlands. But as Albert Sorel, the author of *Europe and the French Revolution* pointed out, the rise of nationalities was to provoke more wars than the ambitions of kings ever did. "Nations' cupidity is fiercer, their triumphs haughtier, and their scorn more insulting than those of princes. They also arouse more bitter and more enduring resentments. Man is no longer affected in his abstract principle, the state or royalty, he is affected in his blood and his race. The passions that used to agitate only a few individuals now reach the masses, and become all the more terrible as the minds of which they take possession are more limited." These passions are found in many societies that have experienced the tumult of history, from Serbia to Rwanda, from Quebec to Korea. In this essay, I shall have to limit myself to cases that are extreme in their radical nature or their duration.

The case of Poland – "a soul in search of a body," Lord Acton wrote in 1862, at a time when it no longer had any territory, having been divided between Prussia, Russia, and the Habsburg Empire – presents an extreme example of a nation that has been deprived of its state because of the cupidity of its neighbors. For the first time, it is said that the arrangement of states is unjust, a people should not be deprived of the ability to constitute an independent community. The Poles' past, as they imagine it to themselves, expresses throughout the depth of their resentment.

A resentment that is still an open wound: Poland

"Poland is not yet dead, so long as we are alive": is there any other people who would put such remarks in its national anthem? Five times Poland was the victim of partitions by its neighbors, in 1772, 1793, 1795, 1815, and then 1939. For over a century, from 1815 to 1918, Poles disappeared as citizens of a sovereign state, and they constantly show foreigners their scars, those of their history. Did Poland deserve such punishment? Or was it the victim of an ongoing crime, an injustice of history? These questions torment its uneasy consciousness. Catholic Christianity has not really taken the measure of its debt to Poland. And this ingratitude has not ceased to keep its resentment alive. Yes, the Poles say, through their heroism and their past sufferings, they deserve a gratitude that they have not yet received. Yes, because Poland has saved Europe four times. Let us see how.

1683: "Here we are on the Danube, lamenting the loss of our horses and the ingratitude of those whom we saved." This remark by Jean Sobieski, king of Poland, paying respect to his army, which had just defended Vienna from the attack of Kara Mustafa, the Ottoman grand vizier, expresses in a premonitory way the resentment of the Poles who, this first time, saved the West from the Turks. Since then, Poland's historical memory has retained, independently of the tragedies constituted by the partitions of its territory, the other heroic moments when it saved the West.

Poland believes that it saved Europe again in 1920, but this time from Bolshevism. The Comintern meeting had, through the mediation of Zinoviev, announced the advance of the Revolution and the triumph of the armies of Lenin and Trotsky. But a miracle took place and Pilsudski's armies halted the Communist offensive before Warsaw. In fact, after Poland recovered its independence in October 1918, its armies, participating in the foreign intervention against the soviet regime, played a difficult role, capturing first Minsk and Belarus, and then entering Ukraine, where, in theory, they were to help the Whites, who were themselves fighting Ukrainian nationalists. But the Whites had no liking for either the Poles or the Ukrainians, whereas the Ukrainians preferred the Reds to the Whites and to the Poles. In this context, Lenin decided that the question was not whether the soviet armies ought to invade Poland after having defeated the Whites, but when and how.

Unhappy with the international arbitration entrusted to Lord Curzon, which set Poland's eastern border, leaving it the region of Bialystok but not the northern part of the Suwalki area, which was inhabited by Lithuanians, Piludski marched on Kiev. But a strong soviet counter-offensive drove him back to Warsaw, where, advised by the French General Weygand, Piludsky stopped the Bolsheviks. This was a great disillusionment for Lenin, who saw that Radek, pointing out that "the workers in Warsaw will see the Bolshevik forces not as revolutionaries but as Russians," had been right to advise him against invading Poland. This campaign put a temporary end to the expansion of Communism in Central Europe. The governments of Western countries were relieved. But did they even express their gratitude?

This ingratitude is found again at the beginning of the Second World War, after Poland was divided up in 1939. Historical memory pays little attention to another of Poland's contributions to the defense of freedom, the role that its armies, which escaped the disaster, played alongside the Allies. First, during the Battle of England, in which the 303rd air squadron shot down a large number of the Luftwaffe's planes; while the "free" Polish forces were the most active troops in all the countries that Germany conquered – Norway, the Netherlands, and free France included. It was, moreover, on this basis that in London General Sikorski developed, during the autumn of 1940, a plan for reorganizing postwar Central Europe under the aegis of Poland.

A year later, when Germany invaded Russia, Poland became the ally of the latter, which had occupied the eastern half of the country in accord with the German–Soviet Pact. Stalin freed Polish prisoners interned in camps (at that time it was not known that in Katyn 4,243 Polish officers had been massacred by Beria, with Stalin's approval), and they began an extraordinary trek that took them from camps in Siberia to Iran, and on to Egypt, where they fought alongside the British. Soon, 50,000 of them were taking part in the Italian Campaign, distinguishing themselves notably at the Battle of Monte Cassino. In his orders, their leader, General Anders, expressed his violent resentment against the German occupiers: "Soldiers, the time for fighting has come. We have *waited for* this moment to *take revenge* on and punish our hereditary enemy." In Cassino, "the Poles, as if under a spell, screamed all sorts of insults against the Germans, sometimes refusing to take cover or be evacuated when wounded. In one day, a battalion of Carpathians was reduced to a dozen men."[19]

Pinning the Order of Bath on General Anders's breast, in the name of George VI, General Alexander declared: "Soldiers of the 2nd Polish Corps, if I were allowed to choose the soldiers I would like to have under my command, I should choose you, the Poles." British, American, French and Italian soldiers had also taken part in this battle.

Simultaneously, during the same summer of 1944, and for the third time, the Poles thought they saved Western Europe from the soviet armies. This was the Warsaw Uprising, which took place in July. As the Poles saw it, by preventing the Wehrmacht from retreating, they slowed the advance of the Russians, who did not, moreover, help the rebels. This tragedy, represented by Andrezj Wajda in his film *Canal*, had its origin in the mutual distrust between the Polish government in exile in London and the one the soviets set up in Lublin. When Russian troops approached, the former took the initiative by promoting an uprising to ensure its sovereignty over the city as soon as it was liberated, while the latter, controlled by the Russians, claimed that it was unable to help the rebels, whereas in truth it intended to take power in Warsaw once the forces of its rival had been crushed.

Whatever the truth is about this event, it exacerbated the Poles' hatred of the Russians, but it did slow the advance of the latter by forcing the Wehrmacht to remain in Warsaw, which allowed the Anglo-Americans to consolidate the liberated zone in France and, later, to reach the Rhine. The Poles in London thought that

[19] Notin, p. 366.

in Yalta a few months later, Churchill and Roosevelt, far from showing gratitude to them for having fought this battle, abandoned the cause of "free" Poland, the Poland that had remained and fought alongside them.

It is not clear that these grievances are well founded in every respect, since, in negotiations among the Allies, Polish leaders showed an intransigence that Churchill considered suicidal. But the Poles' rancor is a fact, even among Poles who did not support the government in exile in London. More concerned about the loss of their eastern territories – which were more Belorussian or Ukrainian than Polish – than about the restoration of Poznan, which had been conquered by Prussia, a year later the Poles felt above all that they had lost their independence once more by becoming a "people's democracy" and a satellite of Soviet Russia.

After the war, the Poles' resentment toward the German "butchers" was extreme – "to avoid the fate of Poland," Pétain and Laval kept repeating to justify their policy of collaboration. And Mussolini noted with indignation at the Germans' behavior in Italy: "They are treating us like Poles."

No country under German occupation experienced a fate as tragic as Poland's, unless it was perhaps Belorussia. There, about six million Poles, including 2,700,000 Jews, fell victim to the Germans: 10 percent of them died fighting. At the same time, the western regions of Poland lost their Polish character and their elites were massacred.

Resentment against the USSR and the regime set up by Moscow overwhelmed the resentment the Poles felt against the Germans. The Katyn massacre, the soviets' denial that they were involved, and then their effort to pin it on the Nazis led to a whole literature on the "assassination" of Poland by the USSR and the Communist regime. This was one of the most incredible manipulations in history. It was only when Gorbachev came to power that the Russians told the truth about Katyn. "We made a mistake," Beria had admitted earlier.

This "assassination of Poland" is all the more plausible because, before 1939, in order to be able to open negotiations with Hitler, Stalin had "liquidated" the Polish Communist Party. Some people believe that 2,700,000 Poles were thus the victims of Soviet Communism between 1918 and 1945, a figure that corresponds – is that merely a coincidence? – to the number of Jewish victims, counted separately, as if the Jews had not been part of the Polish state. In any case, on the basis of recent research, using both Soviet and Polish statistics, the total number of the soviets' victims seems to have been 720,000.[20]

But the Poles' historical memory was soon able to take pride in the heroic battle waged by *Solidarnosc*, which they consider to be the origin of the breakdown of the regimes in Eastern Europe and fall of Communism in the USSR, which once again saved Christian Europe from the Communist menace. Thus the Poles' resentment has continually fed a creativity in the political strategy of disengagement from the USSR that led to an irreversible success. This success was due to *Solidarnosc*, which won a game that no one thought it was up to playing. We can gauge its significance only by comparing this trade union's action with that of leaders of other people's democracies whose efforts were similar but led to tragedies: Budapest in 1956 and Prague in 1968. Once again, "the fate of Europe was played out in Poland."[21]

In this country where hostility to the Russians and to Stalinism made an explosive mixture, in 1964 two militant Communists, Jacek Kuron and Karol Modzelewski, organized a self-administering opposition group that found a wide following in a society that was increasingly detaching itself from its institutions, with the exception of the Catholic Church. In 1970, an abrupt rise in prices triggered giant workers' demonstrations in the Baltic ports. Strikes spread and were renewed, becoming increasingly powerful and involving more and more workers. This reached an apogee in 1980: following the strikes in Gdansk, the regime had to accept the existence of an independent trade union, *Solidarnosc* (Solidarity), which rapidly grew and soon covered the whole country. The "free" union had thus taken over from the Catholic Church, with which it was in agreement, as the Communist Party's main interlocutor. A worker, Lech Walesa, was elected as its leader, while Kuron and Modzelewksi's KOR was its brains. The Polish revolution opened a breach in the closed system of the Communist regimes. This breach was deeper than the wounds opened up and then closed again in Budapest and Prague.

[20] Gurjanov.
[21] Pomian.

Lech Walesa. Did *Solidarnosc* save Europe from Communism?

In Prague, in 1968, faced with general discontent and the regime's failure, the impulse for change had come from the Communist Party itself. The latter had felt the need to reform itself, and had taken the initiative in the movement, thus preserving, in a way, the legitimacy of the system. In fact, twelve years after Budapest, it adopted the language used by Nagy, who had been the first to speak of "a Communism that does not forget man." However, the difference between 1968 and 1956 was that in Budapest in 1956 the movement from above had spontaneously joined itself to a particularly powerful movement from below. This eruption of a second revolutionary center completely disoriented Nagy, who could not imagine that the legitimacy of power could come from anywhere other than the Party and from the Party alone. Paralyzed, he was incapable of standing up to the soviet army or, of course, of fraternizing with the occupying forces.

An essential difference between Poland from 1980 to 1982 and Budapest, Poznan, or Prague, was the fact that the movement owed nothing to the Communist Party, being entirely rooted in the second revolutionary center that had been born in 1964 but had in the meantime been regenerated, so to speak. Since the repression in Prague and especially Gierek's failure to fulfill a second promise of liberalization made in 1970, Poles' illusions about a hypothetical reform from above were dead – dead like the victims of the repression in 1970. What happened in Poland?

As in the USSR, the trade unions were subordinate to the Party. Thus the POUP (Polish Communist Party) imposed its soviet conception of neutralized unions because it subverted their functions and traditional activities (defending workers, organizing strikes, and so on) by transforming them into organs that co-managed the Plan and into channels of communication for the government.

First, the Poles broke the channel of communication. The leadership of the "free" union was no longer named by the Party. Then they elected their own delegates, set up their own institutional structures, instituted their own forms of organization, and finally rejected any dependence on the Party. Thus *Solidarnosc* was born on the ruins of the old union leadership, which wasted away. Thus the Poles went much further than the Hungarian Workers' Councils, in whose creation the union leadership had had a hand, and there were still unions domesticated by the Party. As for competence, *Solidarnosc* did not seek, like factory committees in Russia or, more recently, in Hungary, to institute some form of self-management or co-management of companies. Instead, *Solidarnosc* tended toward a vertical extension of its competence: without presenting themselves as a counter-power; its members challenged certain aspects of the state's functioning, its judicial system, its police, and especially its control over information. As in some sense a substitute for the Catholic Church, and even for the intellectuals, *Solidarnosc* took into account the demands of the society as a whole. *Solidarnosc* extended its competence horizontally to other free "unions" that were being formed.

The recognition of small farmers' right to form a trade union, and not simply an association, showed the slow dismantling not only of a whole system, but of its theoretical foundations, which had been falling apart, piece by piece, because since Gomulka's government in the late 1950s and early 1960s, the principle of forced collectivization had been abandoned. Whence the reaction of the government, which saw the whole of civil society escaping its grasp: in 1981, General Jaruzelski had all the leaders of *Solidarnosc* arrested.

Jaruzelski's defeat of Walesa and *Solidarnosc* was a Pyrrhic victory, because he had no support in the country. For the USSR and the system it incarnated, the events in Poland represented the most serious challenge since 1917. In Warsaw, the Party had lost its real and symbolic power, and it was the army that had stepped in to take its place. This marked the end of an era. The soviets did not intervene to re-establish the Party's authority, and neither encouraged nor restrained the repressive measures taken by Jaruzelski, any more than they had intervened in Hungary to put an end to the furtive emancipation of the Hungarian economy from the obligations of the soviet system. In Central Europe, the system's economic and political bankruptcy intervened in its own way, alongside the war in Afghanistan and an upping of the stakes in matters of armament, to force the USSR to adopt an entirely new policy.

This was the policy incarnated by Gorbachev, who made a radical break with the past. At first, this break took place gradually. The first steps were economic; they failed, and then political steps were taken. Although it has been said that at the time Gorbachev was following in the footsteps of Dubček and the Prague Spring, in fact he was following some of *Solidarnosc*'s procedures: he "cut loose" the local soviets, that is, the municipalities, freeing them from their connection with the Party, and then authorized the trade unions to act independently, thus raising the issue of the Party's leading role.

In Moscow, *Kommunist* wrote that "the Polish experience took on meaning not only for Poland but also for other countries." In an interview with the historian Jacques Levesque, Gorbachev said that he even told Jaruzelski that Poland was "a laboratory and an example for the USSR as well." But above all, it was *Solidarnosc*'s destabilization of the Polish regime that weakened the satellite system and forced the soviet regime to accept these changes. Gorbachev coordinated the stages of perestroika with those of the emancipation of these democracies, so that the changes within the USSR ceased to appear fictitious (as Western spokesmen for the anti-soviet vulgate maintained they were).

After 1989, the end of the soviet regime and the fall of the Berlin Wall allowed Poles rightly to consider that it was their fight that had contributed the most to this authentic revolution: and that Europe owed them its gratitude. But it was Gorbachev whom Europe, including Germany, praised ... which was enough to feed a profound resentment towards Europe. Would France, the eldest daughter of the Church, escape this resentment? The Poles would have to have short memories. To be sure ...

Three times, France was Poland's ally and privileged tutor: in the early eighteenth century, when the marriage of Louis XV to the daughter of Stanislas Leszcznski protected this Catholic country from the threat posed by the Ottomans and by Protestant Prussia; then, after Prussia, Russia, and Austria had partitioned Poland in 1722, 1793, and 1795, Napoleon restored the Grand Duchy of Warsaw, but not Poland, which disappeared in 1815; and finally, when after the First World War a greater Poland was restored at France's initiative. But how many other times did France abandon Poland!

In 1830, when the Poles rose up against the Russians for the first time, and afterward "order reigned in Warsaw," Lamennais stigmatized the French king's cowardice: "May those [of you] who died in the illusion that you were free rest in peace in the grave that one side's crime and the other side's cowardice have dug for you. On this grave there is a cross that says: You shall live again."

1848: once again Poland rebelled; in 1846 the "people's spring" began. "The name of Poland is magical and makes the people of Paris rise up," said Blanqui. It signified, Lamartine added, "the oppression of a human race and vengeance for tyranny." Excited, the political clubs prepared a petition. But the Constituent Assembly responded on 12 May with a decree prohibiting the introduction of any petition into the hall. On 15 May, gathering at the Bastille, the crowd nonetheless began to move, forced its way through the barricades and invaded the Assembly, where Barbès read out the petition. It demanded that an army be sent to Poland, that a billion-franc tax be levied on the rich, and that the army be moved outside Paris. The result was an uproar.

"The Assembly is dissolved!" cried a speaker. Thinking it was dissolved, the demonstrators went to the Hôtel de Ville to set up a new government there. But in the Assembly, there had been a call to arms, and the National Guard arrived. It soon arrested Barbès, Louis Blanc, and Blanqui, who were sentenced to life in prison. "It was a silly mistake on the part of the people,"

Lamartine commented. As for Poland, it had been completely forgotten.

When there was another uprising by the Poles in 1863, Napoleon III showed the same passivity, support for Poland proving incompatible with the alliance France was forming with Russia, but which was finally concluded only under the Third Republic, in 1891. The republicans considered this alliance with an autocratic czar "shameful." People had cried "Vive la Pologne!" when Alexander III visited Paris. The alliance functioned well in 1914, and was confirmed in January 1917 with the finalization of plans for spring offensives: again, it was the Republic that sacrificed Poland to the need to retain the czar's support and to the necessities of war.

If, after the resurrection of Poland in 1918, Warsaw was given help, its abandonment in 1939, during the "phony war," was one of the most shameful episodes in French history. The remains of the Polish army overwhelmed by the Wehrmacht waited in vain for an attack that Gamelin did not dare to launch. Of course, Hitler thought France was terrified by the idea of waging war, but he did not imagine that it would be passive to that point. In 1939, France had followed Great Britain in guaranteeing the Polish borders, and declared war on Germany, which had invaded its neighbor on the east. Four years later, when he went to Moscow, de Gaulle obtained nothing from Stalin: neither regarding the government that would be set up in Warsaw, nor regarding Poland's new eastern border. De Gaulle himself said that he would perhaps have given it up in exchange for the right bank of the Rhine.

Although Paris did welcome Polish intellectuals who had fled the soviet regime's colonization of Eastern Europe after 1945, at the height of the crisis in 1981, the highest French ministers admit ted that they "would do nothing to aid Poland and *Solidarnosc*." Even less: in 1983, Claude Cheysson, Mitterrand's foreign minister, met with Jaruzelski's foreign minister, Czyrek, and to the Poles this looked like another abandonment. Poland had hardly become free again before it had an opportunity to gauge Europe's ingratitude. As much as it had enjoyed Europe's support so long as it was a matter of bringing down Communism, now Europe invoked the economic imbalances between East and West to defer Poland's inclusion into the European Union.

With the end of the soviet regime and the explosion of the former USSR, the long period of powerlessness came to an end and Poles dreamed of resurrection, of a return of Poland's control over Central Europe before it was partitioned in the eighteenth century, dreams that had appeared in August 1940. "Displaced" toward the West, the regions east of the Curzon line that were claimed appeared to be decidedly beyond reach. Warsaw nonetheless kept an eye on Belarus and part of Lithuania. Next, the so-called "Orange Revolution" in Kiev allowed Polish leaders to recover influence in Ukraine (as in 1920) and, furthermore, to weaken Russia. Polish "friends" were also present during the events in Georgia; a situation that recalls that of the influence of the Polish–Lithuanian state in the fifteenth century, which extended from Poznan to the Sea of Azov. In addition, when the Czechs and the Hungarians entered the European Union, Poland was able to play a leading role in challenging the conditions set for their membership.

Above all, to be sure of being integrated into the West and to forestall any offensive return of Russia, it had joined NATO as a precaution, thus putting itself under the American nuclear umbrella even before the European Union took it in. After all, what gratitude to Europe did Poland have to express? Instead, resentment. It owed Europe nothing. And to show it, when Chirac, Schröder, and Putin condemned the American intervention in Iraq, it was Poland that sent troops to Baghdad at the call of George W. Bush.

Resentment within resentment: Austria

Have you seen *1 April 2000*, an Austrian film by Liebeneiner? It dates from 1950. It is a science fiction film that presents itself as a political comedy. It opens with the landing in the year 2000 of an aircraft that has come from who knows where. It carries a delegation representing the Assembly of the Universe. At the latter's request, it has come to judge the Austrian people's guilt for all sorts of crimes of which it is accused. This film represents the malaise that prevailed in the country at that time. It expresses the resentment of a nation against those who were leading it to ask questions about its own behavior.

If an Austrian considers his past, no matter what the period concerned, the mirror reflects in each case his condemnation by other nations, a wound that exudes its pain even though it has become a very small country. What was it accused of in 1950? Of pretending to suffer from amnesia and being victims of the war, without undertaking the slightest de-Nazification, even though the country participated fully in the hostilities, and had not a single deserter. Anyone who speaks of war also speaks of extermination, notably in Yugoslavia, with the participation of Austrian troops. In 1938, immediately after the *Anschluß*, there was a pogrom in Vienna, and then 90 percent of Austria's Jews were exterminated – proportionately more than among the German Jews.

But why should the Austrians feel guilty, when the victorious powers maintained that in 1938 Austria's independence had been violated? The Allies even mentioned this in 1943, in a tripartite declaration of the decision to restore the independence of the country, which consequently asked for reparations in 1945. And Austria was one of the recipients of Marshall Plan aid.

In truth, the Allies' reasons are at the heart of what they thought was their "Realpolitik." Both Roosevelt and Churchill nourished the idea that Nazism was more or less rooted in Germany's Prussian past. Dismantling it by setting up a Southern Confederation to include Austria, Bavaria, and Württemberg would make it possible to neutralize Prussian Germany, that is, northern Germany. Whence the interest in resuscitating Austria, which had always been officially said to have been brought into the Third Reich in violation of international law. In Potsdam in 1945, the victors could say that they had "restored the rule of law."

Of course, in 1950 it was well known that things were otherwise, that 99 percent of Austrians voted for the *Anschluß*, and that they had enthusiastically welcomed Hitler. But henceforth the Austrians, like the Allies, wanted to ignore this. However, that deceived neither the victims of Nazi terror nor part of the Austrian population. The latter knew that this was an imposture. In a significant lapsus, *1 April 2000* shows it: in this country which lent its support to a racist regime, a black and a Jew – or at least, two non-Aryans – detach themselves from the Austrians who are to be judged. The tribunal of the Universe discharges them of imaginary crimes. So Austria also pardons the rest of the world for having misunderstood it. On the screen, the scene immediately opens up and we see a sumptuous palace where dozens of couples in evening dress are dancing to a Strauss waltz. Is this the "good old time" of the Habsburgs, which has come back? No, we have to recall another humiliation.

1919: a caricature in *Kladder Deutsche* represents Austria in the form of a young woman dressed in white, whose head has just been cut off by three sinister, snickering men: Clémenceau, Lloyd George, and Wilson. With her elegant little white-slippered foot, she was trying to pull along a heavy ball labeled "peace." She was vainly looking for her way. Her head, which lies on the ground, is labeled *Deutsch*.

We recall the facts. The defeat in 1918 led to the breakup of the double monarchy, that of the Emperor of Austria and the King of Hungary, under the terms of the Treaty of Saint-Germain. Applying to the victims of the defeated countries the principle of self-determination, the victors took territory away from Austria in order to create Czechoslovakia and Yugoslavia and resuscitated Poland. Not applying this same principle to the defeated countries, it refused to allow the Germans of the former empire, that is, essentially the Austrians, to annex themselves to Germany, despite a vote in the parliament in Vienna in favor of that *Anschluß*, because it would have made Germany even more powerful than it was in 1914 – *géopolitique oblige*.

It remains for us to imagine the anger and trauma felt by Austrians who had been masters and dominators of a vast empire of fifty million inhabitants, henceforth reduced to a small, mountainous territory. A truncated country of 83,000 square kilometers, whereas its former dependencies, among them Hungary and Czechoslovakia, became states that were not only independent but large and full of promising economic prospects.

With its enormous capital, the tiny state soon underwent an economic crisis and political conflicts. Spite regarding the prohibited *Anschluß* grew, and squabbles between the Christian-Democratic and socialists were exacerbated, while an attraction to Nazism increased at the same time that it did in Germany. The assassination of the chancellor, Dollfuss, slowed this development, but the defeat of Chancellor Schuschnigg, who capitulated to Hitler, allowed this *Anchluß* to take place. It was approved by 99 percent of the Austrian population, which gave the Führer a wildly enthusiastic welcome. Even before Nazification was institutionalized – and even before *Kristallnacht*, that anti-Semitic explosion orchestrated in Germany by Goebbels that caused 91 deaths – a pogrom of Jews took place in Vienna, the first explicit expression of Austrians' resentment.

Chancellor Schuschnigg left a record of his interview with the Führer shortly before the *Anschluß* and his own arrest. Hardly had he mounted the grand staircase at the Berghof in Berchtesgaden than Hitler waved away his polite remark on the marvelous view from the picture window in the Führer's living room: "Yes, this is where my ideas ripen," Hitler told him, "but we have not come here to talk about the fine view and the weather." Then, Schuschnigg reports, the Führer grew angry:

> The whole history of Austria was one uninterrupted act of the betrayal of its people by its leaders. This was true in the past, but it was no less true in the present. This historical paradox had gone on too long. It was going to cease. And I tell you, Herr Schuschnigg, I am resolved to put an end to all that. I have set out on the most arduous path ever taken by a German. You can't imagine that you can stop me, even for half an hour? Who knows, perhaps in one night I shall sweep into Vienna like a spring thunderstorm ...

The facts surrounding this quarrel are well known. Neither Britain nor France lifted a finger to preserve Austria's independence; Mussolini had to lend his support, the Austrian state not having either the will or the strength to defend itself. After Chancellor Schuschnigg had resigned, under threat of military intervention, Austria's annexation to the Reich was proclaimed and the Führer was welcomed with a flood of applause throughout the country. The state and the government had been "violated," but the Austrian people had shown its joy. It took part in the war that followed and in the mass crimes that were committed.

"The whole history of Austria was one uninterrupted act of the betrayal of its people ..." This judgement of Hitler's, which has never been noted, accounts for his own strong resentment, as a German Austrian, not only against Social Democrats like Renner, who, like Scheidemann in Germany, accepted the 1919 treaties, and it also accounts for their rancor towards the Hapsburgs. It is not just a matter of Hitler's having joined in 1914, for personal reasons, the Bavarian rather than the Austrian army (he had not responded when the latter called him up for military service). This rejection sprang from wider considerations that were shared by many inhabitants of the Austro-Hungarian Empire.

Of course, the Hapsburgs' power and their way of governing were challenged both by political opponents and subject nationalities – among them Czechs and Slovenes – but the brilliance of the dynasty and of Vienna, its capital, somewhat obscured the connections between the different problems. Then they suddenly all appeared during the sixtieth anniversary celebration of Emperor Franz Joseph's reign in 1908, and they largely account for the resentment felt by some of his subjects, even before the war and the defeats and consequences that followed.

Brigitte Hamann has admirably written that for three hours some twelve thousand persons paraded before their emperor, the marshals marching in front dressed in their uniforms and hats with plumes. The nobles wore splendidly coloured uniforms, while their wives wore elegant summer gowns. Nineteen groups followed, depicting a costumed history of the House of Hapsburg from its ancient foundation by the knights of the time of Maximilian (1459–1519) down to the Tyrolean *Landsturm*, consisting of volunteers who had fought Napoleon. Then came the national groups, one after the other, each emphasizing its ethnic characteristics and parading in the order of their integration into the house of Habsburg: in front, Lower Austria; in the rear, Dalmatia.

This was a gleaming commemoration that confirmed the status of Vienna, the European capital of festivities and music, a city bubbling with intellectual life where Gustav Mahler and Sigmund Freud lived side by side with the Austro-Hungarian Marxists, Otto Bauer and Karl Renner, who were looking for a way to reconcile socialism and nationalities.

However, if we know how this jubilee was organized and how it proceeded, we see that it included in microcosm all the ingredients for the explosion that was smoldering and that was going to blow the empire to pieces.

As soon as the Vienna city council took up the question of organizing these festivities, at the behest of the mayor, who was a member of the Social Christian Party and therefore hostile to the multi-ethnic character of the Empire, the Social-Democrats voted against the allocation of a subsidy, arguing that the regime's achievements did not justify such expenses: the severe repression of the Vienna uprising in 1848, the appeal to the Russian czar to put down the uprising in Hungary, the sovereign's personal defeat at Magenta, and that of the imperial armies at Sadowa, the execution of his brother Maximilian in Mexico – everyone remembered all these failures.

Next, when large companies were invited to bid on the right to sell tickets for seats in the reviewing stands, members of the Social Christian Party protested about the inclusion of a great Jewish shop, Gerngros "because the Jews care little for the Emperor and think only of money." This manifestation of anti-Semitism was not isolated; Gustav Mahler had been harassed in this regard, as had Sigmund Freud, who had been excluded from German nationalist circles, which he supported, and henceforth put his genius in the service of psychological exploration.

Even more, people protested against too great a presence of the high nobility at the head of the procession, which emphasized its opulence, but were told that "at least it didn't cost anything." These criticisms emanated from the middle bourgeoisie, which was then on its way up. It was well aware that the monarch was annoyed by the omnipresence of this high nobility, which contributed so little to the country's economic development.

Next, the Hungarian representatives declared that in their opinion the true anniversary was not the Emperor's jubilee but the celebration the preceding year of the fortieth year of the "compromise" of 1867 that had transformed the Austrian Empire into the Austro-Hungarian Empire. But the Austrians had not participated in this earlier celebration, and the Emperor committed the affront of refusing foreign countries' congratulations on this occasion. The Hungarians decided that they would not take part in the cortege. Although they were subjects of the King-Emperor of Hungary (that is, of Franz Josef), they had refused to allow the construction of a direct rail line linking Vienna and Zagreb, because Croatia belonged to their part of the Empire. They feared that Croatia, which opposed any Magyarization, would develop closer ties with Vienna; thus to go from Vienna to Zagreb, one had to pass through Budapest.

As for the Czechs, who wanted Prague to become a third imperial capital, as Budapest was the second, they planned to go to Vienna to perform a repertory including Shakespeare's *Hamlet*, a

Russian play, and a Czech play – all of them in the Czech language. The mayor, Lueger, informed them that these performances were not compatible with the German character of the city of Vienna. "A Czech theatrical troupe cannot perform in a German city." In response, the Czechs refused to participate in the jubilee.

Finally, it was the Italians' turn to be indignant. Just as at the head of the historical part of the procession the Czechs were reminded of their defeat at the hands of Rudolph of Habsburg, at its end the organizers had planned to play the Radetzky March, a hymn to the Austrian victory over Italian revolutionaries in 1848 at Custozza, a success that was repeated in 1866 by a second victory at Custozza.

Despite its military victories, Austria lost Lombardy, and then Venetia; the Italians "snubbed" the emperor when he visited La Scala in Milan in 1857, the Italian subscribers committing the affront of sending their servants to occupy their seats – an episode that appears in one of the films in the *Sissi* trilogy by the Austrian director Ernst Marischka (1955). A few years later, Franz Joseph was humiliated again by being unable to help his cousin, the king of Naples, against "the bandit Garibaldi, Victor-Emmanuel's rapine, and the insolence of that mob in Paris." Secretly happy that the Hungarians would not participate in the Jubilee, the Croatians almost abstained themselves, the *tableaux vivants* imagined in Vienna representing them as thieves and pillagers. Excuses were made and the tableau cancelled.

A last incident, or rather a rumor, suggested that Vienna's workers were planning to overturn the tribunes, so that thousands of tickets went unsold. When the balance sheet was drawn up, the jubilee had been a financial disaster. But that was not the important thing. Suddenly, on seeing these unknown "compatriots" – these Ruthenians, Romanians, Croatians presented in the satirical magazine *Simplicissimus* as genuine criminals in rags, or at least as barbarians, the Viennese realized that "they were no longer in their own home," and what a multi-national empire really was. They were terrified. But that is still not the important thing. For this procession, Galicia had sent 2,000 persons instead of the 1,000 expected. But Lower Austria had sent only seventy or eighty.

In other words, the Germans of the Empire withdrew from the festivities.

Thus was made blatantly evident the divorce between the German nationalists represented by the Social Christian Party of Lueger and Schönerer, the Austrian ancestors of the National Socialists, on the one hand, and on the other Franz Joseph who, in accord with his policy of nationalities, which was in truth often constrained and forced, refused to consider the Germans as "the people of the state" and named to head the government a Hungarian, Andrassy, as well as a Pole, Goluchovski, or a German, Beust – who was, however, a liberal.

This German rejection was expressed in the Linz manifesto (1882) against an emperor who was reproached for both Olmutz and Sadowa,[22] who forgot that since 1848 the German red, black, and gold flag flew in Vienna, and who had always refused to appeal to German nationalism for fear that it might substitute itself for the dynastic primacy that was his credo. In his view, the only legitimate patriotism was that expressed with regard to the dynasty.

These German nationalists in Austria thus looked to Prussia and dreamed of German domination without a Slavic, or any other, counterweight, finding if necessary "objective" allies (as the Marxists would have said) in the Hungarian nationalists who also despised "these" Slavs, whether they were Croatians or Slovaks. When in 1908, just after the jubilee, Franz Joseph congratulated himself on the successful annexation of Bosnia-Hercegovina, the pan-Germanism that was essentially Austrian (and turned inward, whereas Prussian–German pan-Germanism turned outward) saw in this the arrival of new group of non-Germans who would soil the empire's Germanness. It was therefore not grateful to Franz Joseph, whose only merit in its eyes was that he then strengthened his alliance with Wilhelm II. This context explains the hatred felt by the German pan-Germanists, of whom Hitler was one before 1914, for cosmopolitan Vienna, for Austria and its policies that "did so much harm to the Germans."

The resentment of the Germans of Austria had already exploded when the Czechs tried to impose their language on Germans living

[22] Olmutz (Czech Olomouc) was the site of a treaty between Prussia and Austria in 1848; Sadowa was the site of a battle between Prussia and Austria in 1866 (more commonly known in English as the Battle of Königgrätz), in which Austria was defeated.

in the provinces of Bohemia and Moravia. These Germans were called "Sudetens." We will encounter them again in 1938. A survival or outliers of this past? In 1986, Kurt Waldheim, a former Nazi, was elected president of the Austrian Republic. In 1995, Jorg Haider's neo-Nazi party joined a coalition government, even though Austria had endorsed the European Union's democratic principles. And Slovene immigrants were reminded of the brutality of Austria's earlier ways of treating them. There is still a nostalgia, notably for its victories – over Italy, for example. Every year for several decades, the orchestra of the Vienna Opera has ended its concert on 31 December with the Radetzky March ... A final memory of Austria's last victory: nostalgia or resentment?

France–England: between Siamese twins

If there is a mute resentment in France, it is directed against the English. A family quarrel, a quarrel between relatives, we must remember, because after all France and England are more than twin sisters; they are Siamese twins. For several centuries, during the feudal battles between the Plantagenets/Angevins and the Capetians/Francilians, the unification of the two "nations" was not demanded. It was from the conflict between these "houses" that most of the patriotism of the French and the English was born. At that time, when the monarch in London crossed the Channel, it was said that he was going to wage "his" war, the true enemies of the English then being the Scots. This monarch and his gentlemen spoke the same language as the people of Poitiers, one of his capitals, and he drank wine from Bordeaux. It was with "The Hundred Years War" and the defeats of the Valois at Crécy in 1346 and Agincourt in 1415, immortalized by Shakespeare's plays, that the nature of the antagonism changed: it became nationalist, and was soon incarnated in Joan of Arc, who wanted to "boot the English out of France." However, the dissociation of the two countries in people's everyday lives had already preceded or accompanied these events.

In English schools, pupils resented having to pursue their studies in French, whereas "the gentlemen learned it as soon as they could talk and play with a rattle." The Anglo-Saxon tongue, that of the people, recovered its dominance and with Wycliff it became the language of the Church, with Chaucer the language of literature;

eventually, it once again became the language of the judicial system. Whereas in Guyenne there was no attempt to impose English on the Gascons, in Normandy hostility grew against people who were less and less understood. A symbolic break took place with the marriage of a Lancaster to Isabelle of France: at the final banquet in 1399, the guests refused to be served at the same table: boiled beef and beer for one group, grilled meat and wine for the other, "according to the custom of our countries," they said.

The year 1399 is thus just as important as 1346, 1415, or the appearance of Joan of Arc. The first area of dissension was the notion of "each in his own home," as Thomas Basin put it, or, to use the words of Jean de Montreuil, who thought his country had been invaded: "I hold them [the English] in such abomination that I love those who hate them and hate those who love them." At the end of this war, the country felt itself liberated, though the English kept Calais and Dunkirk.

Religious questions became an occasion for further dissensions, but with eclipses, given the political and religious changes undergone by both countries during the sixteenth century. France's main enemy was then the House of Austria or the Spain of Philip II. The English defeat of the king of Spain's invincible Armada certainly relieved the French, while at the same time producing in them a touch of jealousy because their relief came from a country four times less populous and four times smaller. It is, moreover, from the religious angle that we see what was later called the colonial rivalry between the two countries, at least in Canada, where France settled Catholic colonists to forestall the arrival of Protestants, and in Acadia, where a true religious war took place. In India, it was of course Dupleix's Anglophobia that explains the conflict that broke out there, but "the loss of our colonies," as the French historical tradition presents it, that is, the French defeats at the hands of the British, was not seen in that way on the eve of the French Revolution. When France helped the Americans free themselves from Great Britain, the English experienced this loss, in the nineteenth century, as their most serious and painful setback, which fed their resentment against France. As a result, at the time of the Revolution, and then under Napoleon, one resentment could feed the other, and the rivalry between the two countries grew constantly fiercer.

However, this "little country" took off economically after the Restoration, because it suffered much less from religious conflicts and wars than did the Continent and France in particular, which lost another million people during the Revolution and the Empire. Great Britain carried out its industrial revolution before France did, always moving forward: more urbanized, better equipped, doing away with the subsistence economy and opening up to laissez-faire, to social mobility, to a larger market, its economic boom left the rest of Europe far behind: in 1850, fifty percent of the world's industrial production was English.

From then on, England led the way, with its steamboats, railways, and financiers in the City. Its hegemony was soon challenged by Germany, of course, which caused England to ally itself with France, despite their colonial rivalry, which this time was real, and was manifested in another humiliation for France at Fachoda, in the Sudan, where its garrison had to lower its flag when challenged by Kitchener's armies (1901). The alliance continued during the First World War, but after the armistice Great Britain opposed the French's hegemonic desire to control the right bank of the Rhine, and thus aroused their resentment.

Seen from a distance, this resentment re-established the distrust between the two countries, which should have worked more closely together to oppose Hitler. Only Churchill tried, in vain, to restore trust between the two countries. But the French defeat in 1940, and then the operation in the port of Mers el-Kebir, where the British scuttled the French fleet for fear that it would fall into the hands of the Germans, undermined this trust, de Gaulle being one of the rare persons to dare, angrily, to defend it. Grateful but bitter, the French had to doff their hats to the English, who resisted the Germans beyond all expectations and held on until a very unlikely victory was won. Happy, but a little jealous, the French allied themselves with the British during the Suez crisis. The two colonial powers, for once supporting each other overseas, then suffered a humiliating setback at the hands of the "shameful" alliance that linked the United States and the Soviet Union with Nasser. In the past, when working together, the French and the English had always been successful, especially overseas.

Thus, paradoxically, it was at the darkest moments in their history, when the two countries were allied (1914–1918, 1939–

1945, 1956) – that French mistrust of the English was the greatest and England's Francophobia the strongest; to see this, one has only to read the contemporary press. It is in France that resentment against the English is the most deeply rooted, and it is in France that all the anti-English stereotypes aroused by the memory of Joan of Arc and Napoleon were born or reproduced, especially during the nineteenth and twentieth centuries.

During the eighteenth century, the French were already accusing the English of paying other people to fight their battles. This accusation was revived during the First World War, whereas in reality England lost almost as many men as France, and not, as has been said, to save its empire, but on the Somme and in Flanders as well. In Jean Renoir's 1937 film *La Grande Illusion*, the English prisoners are shown with tennis rackets – a way of suggesting that they are not real soldiers. In *Alerte en Méditerranée*, made in 1938, French sailors sing anti-English, not anti-German songs. The French commanders of the ship treat the English and the Germans in the same way, even though at that date England was France's ally and Germany its enemy.

Once war was declared, the resentment felt by Pétain and Weygand was fed by England's reluctance to land a substantial expeditionary corps and its refusal to use its air force. "The English are abandoning us," just as during the "phony war" the French abandoned the Poles. At Dunkirk, the French like to think only the English escaped, but in fact a good third of the evacuees were French. In short, when the French fleet was sunk at Mers el-Kebir, the resentment reopened all the old wounds.

And then Churchill, facing the soviet threat, proposed in 1946, in Zurich, that Europeans unite. The French turned up their noses; how could such a proposal not have come from them? And that led, via the Monnet plan, to the Schuman Declaration, which put the French and West German steel and coal industries under joint control and paved the way for the emergence of the European Union. Then the English pointed out that the three heralds of this new Europe – Gasperi, Adenauer, and Schuman – represented countries that had, respectively, embraced Fascism, Nazism, and collaboration. Now the English were giving lessons in morality – a new example of insolence added to all the past grievances. Their dominance would have become intolerable had they not, after the victory of 1945, lost part of their power.

The British had been the masters of business and the railways; they had invented football and rugby, as well as lawn tennis and week-ends, established the dominance of beefsteak, roast beef, rump steak, and the Beatles, and now they were, once again, the first to show signs of decadence. Jealousy or resentment?

Germany–France: the alternation of resentments

"All French people feel resentment against foreigners," Benjamin Constant wrote in his *Journaux intimes* in 1816. That did not prevent the French from also having "short memories," as Pétain noted in 1941. We might rather say "selective memories," but are the French the only ones?

In 1948 President Vincent Auriol, unctuously commemorating the tercentenary of the Peace of Westphalia, sought to recall the reattachment of Alsace to France even more than the end of the Thirty Years War. Although at that time French resentment against Germany was still strong, and fed by an age-old contention, it did not occur to Auriol that he was reviving Germans' resentment against France, a resentment that was much older – but who knew about that in France? France's participation in the Thirty Years War (1618–48) had marked its exit from the traditional rivalries among "houses" and the emergence of a *national* resentment. The annexation of parts of Alsace was the point of departure for a dispute that later grew steadily more bitter. The French monarchy henceforth appeared to be a "predatory machine" of which Germany was the chief victim. After the three bishoprics, annexed in 1559, came Besançon, an imperial free city, annexed in 1678, parts of Flanders, and then the "rape" of Strasbourg, all of which were contemporary with the campaigns of Louvois, who was an adept of the scorched-earth tactics that started in the Palatinate and whose horrors exceeded even those of the Thirty Years War. In Germany, the Peace of Nimwegen was known as *Nimmweg*, the kidnapping, and the Treaty of Ryswick, where Germany kept Strasbourg, as *Reissweg*, or "tearing away," and the Treaty of Utrecht (1713) as "Treaty of Injustice."

France had thus become Germany's hereditary enemy. But there was no awareness of this at the court in Versailles, which hardly cared about the Peace of Westphalia or the Germans, regarding the battle against Spain and England as having priority. The neglect and scorn with which Germany was treated only added to its resentment. Louis XIV's condescension in considering whether he should become emperor humiliated Germany, because the emperor was elected. And France diminished the German peoples at a time when they took pride in having defended Christianity against Ottoman attack at the siege of Vienna in 1683. With the Revolution of 1789, the two societies established relations for the first time, if only through the mutual support of the "philosophes" of the Enlightenment – d'Holbach, Diderot, Grimm, Klopstock, Hölderlin.

But there was no revolutionary situation on the other side of the Rhine. In the war that began in 1792, although the Battle of Malmy constituted, in Goethe's view, "a turning point in world history" for Germany, the so-called "revolutionary" war was transformed into a new French occupation followed by conquests. Napoleon imposed a vassal system, an annexation, and then a transformation of the left bank of the Rhine into French departments. Next, the 1803 *Reichsdeputationshauptschluss*, the final law passed by the imperial diet, dissolved the ecclesiastical principalities, most of the free cities, and the small states. Finally, the creation of the Confederation of the Rhine in 1806 – which Napoleon called "my confederation" – soon extended as far as the Elbe. With its 130 departments, France dominated Westphalia and Bavaria and integrated them into its territory.

Although it accepted the Napoleonic *Code civil*, Germany felt humiliated, ransomed; Fichte called for rebellion. By proceeding to make conquests, the French Revolution not only perverted its principles but also put an end to what remained of German unity: thus priority was given to reconstituting the latter by occupying the Rhineland. The resentment of the Germans was expressed in Heine's poetry, to which Alfred de Musset replied: "You won't get your German Rhineland." A categorical imperative, the unification of Germany was achieved when Prussia put it on its program and Bismarck defeated Austria-Hungary in 1866 and France in 1871. Germany finally recuperated the provinces "torn away" by the Peace of Westphalia. But its resentment was revived when France took Alsace-Lorraine back in 1918. The German "program" in 1914 had foreseen the "return" of Luxemburg, Franche-Comté, and part of Burgundy, so that the

Reich would once again have its borders at the time of the Holy Roman Empire in the age of Sigismund. These objectives were also those of Hitler and National Socialism, which through its victory over the French Third Republic in 1940 reincorporated Alsace and Lorraine, while expecting further conquests once the Reich had defeated England and the Soviet Union. But history decided otherwise.

As for French resentment, before it became anti-German it was directed against Prussia. In the eighteenth century, the king of Prussia was the first target. During the War of the Austrian Succession (1740–1748), Louis XIV was allied with Frederick II, who abandoned him once Silesia had been annexed. As a saying of the time put it, "France fought for the king of Prussia." Prussia participated in all the coalitions against France during the Revolution and the Empire, despite the "compensations" granted by Napoleon in 1803–1805 to counterbalance his annexations. French resentment increased on seeing the help Prussia gave the European coalition during Napoleon's retreat from his Russian campaign, especially at the Battle of Leipzig. Prussia clearly emerged as the rising power that, with England, desired the ruination of France. The fame of German writers, philosophers and artists, such as Schiller, Goethe, Hegel, Beethoven, Schumann, Brahms, Mendelssohn, and soon Wagner, now fed France's resentment against its cousin beyond the Rhine. In reaction, while admiring Wagner, Debussy wanted to be called a "French musician." At the same time, in the sciences Koch competed with Pasteur and the School of Medicine in Paris.

The fact that during the revolution of 1848 Bismarck denounced "French-style anarchy" and that his diplomacy stymied that of Napoleon III further fed the hereditary enemy syndrome after the loss of Alsace-Lorraine and the siege of Paris in 1870–1871. "Eat your bread," a mother told her son before 1914, "at least the Prussians won't get that much." It was only after the First World War that resentment was directed against Germans rather than Prussians. During the Second World War, it was Germans, not Nazis, that leaders and public opinion blamed, whether they were for or against collaboration. Only the left-wing Catholics associated with the review *Esprit* and a few politicians really respected this distinction, the Communists speaking instead of the battle "against Fascism."

On the eve of the Second World War, the suffering endured because of the Occupation and then the discovery of the death camps exacerbated the resentment, which was now directed against all Germans, the Nazis and their accomplices, military or civilian. However, little by little, a twofold change can be observed. Whereas the majority of the French bore the stigmata of the Occupation, those who had been prisoners – not the deportees, of course – had a more favorable view of Germany, because they had not been mistreated, a feeling that was expressed by films such as Henri Verneuil's *La Vache et le Prisonnier*, starring Fernandel (1959) and André Cayatte's *Le Passage du Rhin*, starring Charles Aznavour (1960). Besides, having been divided into four parts (East and West Germany, Austria, and Berlin), the former Reich no longer appeared menacing, and it was the Americans or the Soviets who appeared to pose a threat: de Gaulle embraced Adenauer in reconciliation, a gesture that Mitterrand and Kohl repeated in Verdun. Moreover, thanks to the Monnet Plan and Robert Schuman, economic relations between the two countries were developing, and a certain complicity was appearing between the "managers" on both sides of the Rhine. Finally, in France, there was an increasing tendency to blame Vichy for crimes that had long been attributed to the Germans and to them alone.

There is no doubt that Marcel Ophuls's film *The Sorrow and the Pity* (1969) and Robert Paxton's book *Vichy France* contributed to the shifting focus of this resentment. Except, of course, among the descendants of the victims of Nazism, even if official Germany has never ceased to express its repentance for the crimes committed during the Nazi period. In 1931, Briand and Laval dreamed that their two countries would "bury the hatchet" of war. At the dawn of the twenty-first century, one can say that this has finally happened. And yet the re-unification of Germany in 1989 made a shiver run up the backs of those who, like François Mauriac, said that they liked Germany so much that they'd prefer to have several of them.

4

Post-Colonization and Communalism

At the turn of the century, the renewed violence of resentments proves – were proof needed – that in history the page is never turned and that it is pointless to speak, like Fukuyama, of "the end of history." Whether it is a matter of the return of Islam or the reactivation of Jihad, of fire smoldering among Native Americans or the perverse effects of the failure of Soviet Communism, all these phenomena have seemed surprising, if not unpredictable.

The colonial problem did not end when colonies became independent, anymore than the gigantic population movements that accompanied independence. In Andean America, for instance – lest one forget – it was the colonists who won independence from Spain, not the natives from the colonists. In Europe, we are constantly confronted by the consequences of colonization and the judgments made regarding it. The failure of the soviet experiment has not put an end to anti-imperialist ideas that were, in part, its origin, or even to the nostalgia that the disappearance of colonialism has elicited here and there. Are these phenomena connected? In any case, if no common thread can be discerned, it remains that through the resentment to which earlier ordeals gave rise this past is as present as the present, and often drives it. Let us try to determine one of the itineraries of the resentment against the former Arab, and then the Atlantic, slave trade, up to the present time.

Black is beautiful

The African world also had its Spartacus. His name was Ali ibn Muhammad, also known as Sahib al-Zanj, that is the master of the Zanj, most of whom were Bantu-speaking people brought as slaves from East Africa, especially to Mesopotamia (modern Iraq), to make arable the nitrous lands of Shatt al-Arab. They were divided into groups of 500 to 5,000 workers, cooped up and fed on flour, semolina, and dates. The first uprisings in 689 and 694 failed. The one led by Ali ibn Muhammad against the Arabs lasted from 869 to 883, and was contemporary with Charles the Bald and the Norman invasions in the West. The insurrection seized control of half a dozen cities, including Basra, and finally set up a state. From its capital, al-Mani'ah, it dominated the whole region of the canals before it was crushed by the future Abbasid caliph Al-Mutadid. Ali ibn Muhammad was killed, and his close associates beheaded.

This triumph over the slaves was celebrated in Baghdad as a great victory. The regent who won it received the title "Al-Nasir li din Allah" – he who supports the religion of God. This "master of the Zanj" had embraced several religious doctrines; he was also a poet, and his revolt grew out of his humiliation. In his own way, he adopted the tone of Al-Jahiz of Basra, a prose writer who was also partly of African descent. In his *Risalat mufakharat al-sudan 'ala al-bidan* (Superiority of the Blacks to the Whites), he defended the Zanj against the Arabs, emphasizing their qualities: "strong, courageous, cheerful, and generous, and not because of the weakness of their intelligence or their indifference to the consequences of their acts. [...] And then, the only ones whom people knew about were those who had been reduced to slavery ..." He concluded that "the colour black is beautiful in nature, in the animal realm, and among men as well. This black colour is not a punishment, but the result of natural conditions: grasshoppers are green on leaves, lice are black on the head of a man when he is young, and white when his hair turns white."

This insurrection "put an end to the sole attempt made in the Muslim world to transform family slavery into colonial slavery,"[23] that is, by making captives into forced laborers. In relation to the

[23] Alexandre Popovitch.

Arab or African slave trade, the Atlantic slave trade had one essential distinctive feature: not only brutal uprooting, but also being transported across the sea, under inhuman conditions, toward unknown lands. Even before these unfortunate victims were cooped up and put to forced labor, their ordeals and the sufferings they endured constituted a kind of violence that history had seldom known before.

It remains that in Black Africa the Zanj, like other African peoples, have remembered the wound inflicted by the violence connected with the slave trade.

Given that today colonization and then independence have covered over this distant past, and that multinational imperialism imprisons and paralyzes African mixed (Christian, Muslim, polytheistic) societies, historians of Africa hesitate to discuss that past. It was a film camera that reminded us of the resentment in the Wolof areas of Senegal, a resentment that the common people, the Ceddo, feel against the dominant Islam. In Ousmane Sembène's 1977 film *Ceddo*, these people defend their freedom against the Muslim religion, colonial commerce, and Catholicism all at once. The Catholic priest who is trying to convert slaves watches passively as the chief's advisors are indoctrinated by the representatives of Islam, who first seize spiritual power and then temporal power. The Ceddo rise up and kidnap the chief's daughter. She shows neither hostility nor liking for her kidnappers. An armed conflict between the Ceddo and the new rulers breaks out. The princess is taken back from the kidnappers and is now supposed to marry the new chief, a Muslim, but instead she shoots him. Thus, a young, beautiful woman embodies determination and freedom. She also defends the identity of her people, who will pervert customs brought in from elsewhere. A courageous film in a country where the elites are Muslim.

The fate of the victims of the Atlantic slave trade naturally leads us to inquire into their reactions once they arrived in America. In the Caribbean and in the colonies that were to become the United States, these slaves were often moved to desperate acts, self-mutilations and suicides. Others tried to escape or rebelled. Escapes were more likely to be successful in sparsely populated tropical regions like Brazil, Surinam, or Jamaica. Some of the rebels were finally able to gain independence, as in the case of Haiti, but most of the revolts were crushed. For example, Nat Turner's 1831 rebellion in the United States: it was put down after having sown panic in Virginia, where a hundred slaves killed sixty people in twenty-four hours before being killed themselves. And there were innumerable individual revolts. In most of these colonies, festivals provided the institutional framework for the survival of songs, dances, and other African musical expressions. Organizing these festivals became the matrix for a kind of counter-power exercised by the man called the "governor," whose pre-eminence the whites accepted, because he was often a descendant of a king, and it was he who negotiated with the master. The latter often brought delinquent slaves before this "governor," thus diverting the slaves' resentment towards members of their own community.

As for converted slaves, they retained their heritage better in Catholic countries, where it gave rise to a variegated syncretism, than in Protestant countries where blacks were accepted as members of the church only insofar as they had learned the elements of the faith. Thus Protestant evangelization led to the disappearance of a large part of their African traditions. Were white people really given souls? That is a question Frantz Fanon asked in *Peau noire, masques blancs* (1952).[24] Was this a response to what Gunnar Myrdal wrote in *An American Dilemma* (1944), namely that in the United States a black man was first of all an American? And what about the French Antilles?

In Martinique, one of the first things the Second Republic did in 1848 was to make "the whole population French citizens, in fraternity." The Republic had been proclaimed on 25 February, and freedom and universal suffrage was established on 5 March. On 27 April, the newly freed slaves were given or forced to accept the status of citizens, that is, a nationality and an identity, at the same time that the decree abolishing slavery was promulgated. Concretely, the decree provided an amnesty for slaves "whom horror of servitude had led to flee, and to fugitive slaves who have occupied lands."

In short, on reading Myriam Cottias's analyses, we see that the French, in granting amnesty to the slaves, forgot how humiliating the latter's fate was. More than that: violence having broken out on 22 May, the day on which emancipation was recognized, the

---

[24] [Translator's note: Published in English as *Black Skin, White Masks*, trans. Richard Philcox.]

expected decree promulgating the abolishment of slavery finally
arrived, "the proposition of social peace that was based on forgetting inequalities and the past became a forgetting of the events of
22 May." The violence of the riots had to be forgotten, and not
slavery, the amnesty becoming amnesty for the rioters. The mass
celebrated on 8 June 1848 was dedicated to the victims of 22 May,
not for the crime committed against the slaves, but for the crime
committed by the slaves, to calm their passions.

Cyrille Bissette, a free man of colour, had been banned from
French territory a few years earlier for having written that "he
would never pardon his tormentors." Since then "he does not deny
his profound resentment graven there by the way he was treated,"
but he noted with pleasure that this feeling had faded because
France had recognized the iniquities of which he had been the
victim. It remains that in Martinique and in Guadaloupe the
working conditions ("a second kind of slavery"), the salaries, and
the colonists' racism perpetuate the memory of the past. "The vain
African," the whites exclaim, "death to the whites!" the blacks
respond, and these cries punctuate the history of the Caribbean.
It was to be a very long time before slavery was not only formally
abolished but also explicitly condemned "as a crime against
humanity": an act of Parliament achieved thanks to the eloquence
of Christiane Taubira, the representative from French Guiana,
who could then cry that she was "proud to be black."

"I'd like to see the day when my people will be proud to be
black and will acknowledge their colour with dignity," wrote
Kenneth Clark in *Dark Ghetto*. In the United States, in the early
1950s, that day was still distant, even if some churches expressed
solidarity with the civil rights movement led by Martin Luther
King, the hero of non-violence. Independently of the aggressiveness of the members of the Ku Klux Klan, in the Deep South
everyday racism was common. In every conflict that broke out, it
was always the black man who was at fault, as we clearly see in
Clarence Brown's film *Intruder in the Dust*. "So much the worse
or so much the better if blood has to be shed, but everything is
possible," people said at that time in black communities, embit-
tered by so much ingratitude and cruelty. Hadn't they, beginning
with Revolutionary War, served as medical orderlies, saved lives,
showed as much civic sense and devotion as anyone? Hadn't they
done their duty in two world wars? But it was after the First World

War, in 1919, that the largest number of blacks was lynched in the South: seventy. Some of them were still wearing their military uniforms. That year there were twenty-five riots. In 1941, blacks were not allowed to attend a banquet in support of the war effort. Exasperation with these humiliations steadily grew, to the point that Eisenhower became the first president since Lincoln to publicly condemn the excesses of segregation. But, he explained to Paramount News, "that is because it gives America a bad image abroad." At the time, the Cold War was at its height. Naturally, initial steps were taken to limit segregation, but resentment and powerless waiting led to both transfigurations and explosions: the 1960s and 1970s were decisive.

One of the first, extreme solutions, conceived by black people around 1900, was a return to Africa. This idea was developed by Marcus Garvey, who proposed the creation of a kind of black Zionism on the model of the Jews scattered over the world, so that 400 million blacks could finally form a nation. Its flag was to be red like the blood shed in the course of history, black like the color of the skin of which blacks ought to be proud instead of ashamed, and green like hope. Would it be Africa? "No" was the answer for James Baldwin and others who made pilgrimages there and returned disenchanted. Back in the United States, these pilgrims felt more American than African. "Have a nation before having a God," people had repeated. That is what happened in the European colonies, many of which became independent, not only in the Caribbean – for instance, Trinidad and Tobago, Jamaica – but also in tropical Africa. But in the United States, because it seemed impossible to imagine that blacks could be sovereign in any state whatever, joining Islam seemed to some a solution.

These Black Muslims, who supported "black power," said "the whites' time is over ... Why integrate ourselves with the moribund?" Active, functioning as a community, they adopted a mode of behavior in conformity with Islam's most puritanical rules: they didn't drink or smoke, and they produced films that revealed all their virtues but were so boring that their cinemas were soon empty. Nonetheless, the real disillusion came from the Muslim world – in this case, from the Arab world – which they hoped would help defend their rights at the UN or elsewhere, the kind of help Tunisian Muslims got when they challenged French policies.

But the Arab world, which was at that time led by Nasser, was trying to get American help in resisting Anglo-French "colonialism," notably in Suez. Thus the Arabs lost interest in the Muslim community that had hoped to graft itself onto a world that would help it free itself.

In 1957, a serious incident occurred in Little Rock (Arkansas). The governor had used the state National Guard to prevent black students from enrolling in white schools. President Eisenhower sent in US Army troops to ensure that the black students were able to enter the schools. The governor then decided to close the public schools, but the Supreme Court declared this illegal. After blacks and whites took part in the peaceful "March on Washington" in 1963, Malcolm X, a black Muslim leader, was assassinated. A few years later, the non-violent leader Martin Luther King was also assassinated. However, although violence spread and exploded in numerous cities in the early 1970s, something different was going on in the depths of society.

In Richard Brooks's 1955 film *Blackboard Jungle* we see for the first time a group of black and white students smash their teacher's 78 r.p.m. records and substitute for them a 45 r.p.m. recording of "Rock around the Clock," rock and roll being opposed to jazz the way the teenagers are to their elders. In this film also we see a black, Sidney Poitier, playing one of the main roles. The greatest success in the history of music coincided with the first accepted integration of blacks into the white world, the resentment expressed by both coinciding with young people's resentment against their elders. Rock and roll includes elements of both black culture and white culture, the music thus contributing to the process of the cultural integration of blacks into the American nation. Paul Yonnet observed that "whereas with Chuck Berry blacks sang hymns to the automobile, to leisure, to flirting, expressing their desires in symmetry with Elvis Presley, young blacks appropriated black 'sexuality' by expressing erotic attitudes." The "old blacks" of New Orleans and the Deep South on the one hand, and the KKK on the other immediately expressed their anger. The spread of rock and roll humiliated them. Alongside this musical explosion, the protest movement changed in nature as well. Unlike the Black Muslims, the Black Panthers were black only in name. They did not consider themselves blacks but revolutionaries. Among them – and I met some – there are as many whites as blacks,

Asians, and "Latinos." They are Marxist-Leninists who consider themselves Americans whose origins don't matter. The double assassination of Malcolm X and Martin Luther King led them to organize urban protests in which, in a very disciplined way, they paraded in perfect order, in rhythm and fists raised. In 1970, their rise in power worried the White House. Their movement was crushed. Their leaders went to Algiers, like Eldridge Cleaver, and other Third World combat sites. It is true that organized violence, revolutionary or not, had failed. But in thirty years, what changes had taken place! Through their prayer meetings, silent marches, and raising their fists after winning at the Olympic Games, blacks had acquired, after a hard-fought struggle, their place in American society. They flaunted these victories by putting their loveliest women, like Angela Davis, at the head of their parades. What allure: black is beautiful.

This became the slogan for a community that had transformed its resentment into triumphal pride. It had raised the stone over its tomb and saw the sunlight once again. The political and cultural shock of those years had led the American government to take certain steps: successively, the introduction of a quota in the bureaucracy and the armed forces, and then Affirmative Action, a form of positive discrimination intended to overcome disadvantages related to race. The result was that to the small black middle class that already existed, especially in New York, was added a cultivated elite composed of jurists, university professors, and others. Blacks soon were elected mayors in Chicago, San Francisco, and even in New York in 1989. In 2008, a black, Barack Obama, was elected president of the United States. However, black society continues to include immense pockets of poverty, and racial incidents and riots continue to occur.

For blacks, the idea of receiving an indemnity for the slavery of which they had been the victims was a promise they had soon forgotten. It dated from 1865, when General William Sherman allegedly promised each family of freed slaves forty acres and a mule to plow it.

It was the Black Panthers who, during the 1960s, reminded people of this promise. In their ten-point program, they demanded that this promise be kept, reviving blacks' resentment and hopes. In support of their demand they referred to the example set by West Germany, which had paid indemnities to the children of Jews

Black is beautiful. Smiling, blacks raise their fists at the 1968 Olympic Games.

who had been deported to the death camps. Since 1989, Congressman John Conyers has introduced a bill to create a commission to study this question. Basing themselves on the principles of Affirmative Action, black lawyers sued the still existing companies whose capital had originally been derived from labor of the slaves who had worked for them and who still lived in the area. "Slavery has left marks on today's society and has condemned the black population to poverty, unemployment, and a lack of education. That is what we want to set right," one of the lawyers explained. Repentance? No, reparations!

When a large number of representatives of African and Arab states met in Durban in 2001 to demand excuses and reparations from those who had been involved in the slave trade, the European Union presented its apologies for past crimes, but rejected any idea of compensation. Moreover, the African representatives were circumspect and divided, because, for example, in the former Dahomey (now Benin) the Yoruba people were the victims of the Fon, and in Gabon, it was still common for children to be sold into slavery. Unlike black Americans who were trying to obtain indemnification for crimes committed in the past, 80,000 Sioux were able obtain compensation. Thanks to good lawyers, Australian aborigines were also able to acquire civil rights.

The resentment of the colonized

It is among the indigenous population of the Americas that social or political claims, connected or not with resentment, took the most varied forms during the 1980s, from the simple demand for reparations among the Mapuches in Chile to the revolutionary terrorism of the *Sendero Luminoso*. In Bolivia, when multinational companies carved up the country, they provoked an Indianist reaction that took power democratically. To gauge the importance of this Indian awakening, which has also occurred in other Andean countries, we must recall that the Latin American independence movements connected with the names of Bolivar and San Martin, the "liberators," were independence movements led by colonists against Spain, not indigenous movements. Moreover, in Peru, the natives sided with the Spaniards, because the Crown and the Church were trying to limit the power of the conquistadors and their descendants. Should we go so far as to say that when

independence came in the 1830s, the Indians' situation worsened?
To do so would be to frame the problem in the wrong way, because
purely Indian areas are rare and mixed-race populations are
broadly prevalent. Pure creoles of European origin are in the
majority only in Chile. "We are all mixed-race," Peruvians like to
say, although there exist large Indian areas in the mountains. In
Bolivia, mixed-race people "play the role of whites" in relation to
the Indians.

In any case, although genuine social and racial conflicts are
connected with the degree of inter-breeding – some people have
spoken of a "pigmentocracy"[25] – an old resentment nonetheless
remains against the first conquistadors. In a famous book, *The
Vision of the Vanquished* (1971), Nathan Wachtel has shown how
this resentment was expressed in the native folklore; more recently,
Federico Garcia filled the cinemas in Lima, Cuzco, and Ayacucho
with his film *Tupac Amaru*: the audience was mainly Indian or
mestizo. In this film, the leader of a final Indian insurrection,
Tupac Amaru II, is executed in 1781 "because of a Spaniard's
betrayal." The defeat of Tupac Amaru II had many other causes,
notably the internal divisions among the Indians. But this scenario
reveals the guilt felt by the Peruvian intellectuals who have assembled the records of the conquest. Their analyses, expressed from
an anti-colonialist point of view, have influenced the programs of
revolutionaries whose action long remained only verbal. By moving
to action, Shining Path (the Peruvian Communist Party, also
known as *Sendero Luminoso*) put them on the spot, because it
was inspired by Maoism's harshest mottos and practices, in the
manner of Pol Pot.

During the 1980s one could read, at an altitude of 3,000 meters
in the Sierra de Cuzco, a sign in fiery letters: "Down with the
Albanian traitors." This was a warning issued by the Maoist
Shining Path International stigmatizing the Albanian regime for
having detached itself from China, the new leader of the worldwide revolution. According to the Marxist Mariategui, Peru had
remained a colonial country, and while Shining Path encouraged
nativism, it was in reality run by mestizos. Its leader, Abmaël

---

[25] In the local vocabulary, the pigmentocratic system defines all the crossings: *mestizo* (Spanish-Indian), *castizo* (mestizo-Spanish), *mulato* (Spanish-
black), *morisco* (Spanish-mulatto), *albino* (Moorish-Spanish), etc.

Guzman, belonged to the national education administration and was originally a philosophy professor specializing in Kant. He expressed his hatred for Deng Xiaoping by displaying hanged dogs in trees, and his scorn for Moscow for having betrayed world revolution. His only foreign associates in Shining Path International – the "Fourth Sword," after Marx, Lenin, and Mao – were the Maoist Communist Party of Colombia and revolutionary groups, notably Trotskyist ones, such as Tupac Amaru in Peru, or groups elsewhere in Latin America that took their inspiration from Fidel Castro and Che Guevara.

Like his intellectual models, Guzman was looking for efficacy: faced by the "colonizers" of Lima and the coast, he practiced terrorism the way the Algerian National Liberation Front practiced it, by attacking the symbols of power – such as military barracks and ministries – and organizing a series of spectacular attacks, such as one that cut off the capital's electricity. At the same time, he was sufficiently rooted in the Ayacucho region to feel "like a fish in water," to use the Maoist formula, this region being his Yenan. In this territory that he controlled, he practiced state terror of Leninist-Stalinist type, taking draconian measures to "starve the cities." Thus villagers who, in order to survive, continued to deliver fruit and vegetables to the cities were executed. Caught between this policy of terror and the repression carried out by the army, which was frequently called in to help, the people living there didn't know what to do.

In less than a dozen years, Shining Path's uprising had caused 69,000 deaths. Concluding that China's adoption of a market economy and the failure of the Sandinista revolution in Central America had compromised the future of worldwide revolution, and hence that "armed struggle is no longer viable," Guzman let himself be arrested in 1992. His forces, which were associated with those of the Tupac Amaru Revolutionary Movement, were responsible for 59 percent of the dead, and the army for 28 percent, the cause of the remaining victims not being identified. A truth and reconciliation commission created in 2001 and organized by collectives more than by the state is trying to restore a voice to a political, post-colonial, post-revolutionary function.

It remains that the Shining Path experience strengthened the recovery of Indians and the least creolized lower classes, those that did not try to pass themselves off as creoles. And that, in these Andean countries as a whole, anti-colonialism assumed the guise of anti-imperialism, the alliance between the ruling classes and the United States being the common denominator of the general resentment. In its most extreme form, just as Fidel Castro reached out to Nikita Khrushchev in the early 1960s, Hugo Chavez, in Venezuela, is now reaching out to Iran's Ahmadinejad.

Although there is no doubt that Venezuela's petroleum resources have made its people concerned about the flight of dividends derived from this national source of wealth – as is also the case for natural gas in Bolivia – the vigilance of its former leaders had already played a role in the creation of OPEC, the cartel formed in 1960 with the Arab oil-producing states. The Venezuelan people's resentment against the United States is older, oil having been discovered there only in 1922. It dates from the "crisis" of 1902, which in Venezuela marks the transition from the hegemony of Europe to that of the United States. Theodore Roosevelt was then conducting a crusade against Venezuelan debtors on behalf of all the country's creditors. Contemporary with the expedition against the Chinese "Boxers," which was led by Wilhelm II, this intervention was undertaken in the name of the Monroe Doctrine "to protect the country from European intervention" (*sic*), and by virtue of moral principles. Americans acted differently from Europeans.

Up to that point the British had not given any ideological cast to their economic domination in Latin America. They had not gone there, as they did to Africa, "in the name of civilization": they were doing business as usual. The Americans, on the contrary, wanted to export their native Puritanism, this demand for virtue that is at the origin of their independence. They wanted to lead the South Americans toward a "proper" management of their affairs, which immediately struck Latin-Americans as a hypocritical trick to take control of their budgets. The goal of American didactic moralism was to perpetuate American domination, since it is true that the master always retains a certain ascendancy over the pupil.

Practicing the "big stick" policy, the United States had "liberated" Cuba from Spanish domination; in the name of its security, it controlled Panama, which it had seized from Colombia; later on, the United States frequently intervened in the politics of the small banana republics of Central America. Still later, as Noam Chomsky has shown, the generous funding given by the US State Department and the CIA to governments in Central and South America was not unrelated to the crimes against humanity committed in those countries. This aid was given in the name of the battle for democracy, against subversion, and by virtue of the moral rigor that American policy claimed to embody. "Slave morality says 'no,' and it is this 'no' that gives birth to values," Nietzsche wrote. So long as he cannot take action, "the resentful man" ruminates on an imaginary revenge. We find these characteristics among colonized peoples.

Nehru combined sarcasm with a certain admiration of the oppressor. "One of the most remarkable things about English domination in India is that the greatest evils it has inflicted on this people are given the outward appearance of gifts from heaven: railways, the telegraph, the telephone, radio, and the rest were welcome; but we must not forget that their primary objective was to strengthen British imperialism on our soil by permitting a tightening of its administrative grip and the conquest of new markets for the products of British industry. However, despite all my resentment at the presence and the conduct of foreign masters, I had no resentment against the English as individuals. Deep in my heart, I rather admired that race." The expression of his scorn corresponds to the humiliation:

> Completely loyal to His British Majesty, we did not feel ourselves worthy of untying his shoe laces (...) but the Englishman in India always frequented the same small clan (...) a class that exuded a singular boredom and narrowness of mind. He soon succumbed to a kind of intellectual and cultural torpor. On leaving his office at the end of the day, he took a little exercise, then went to find his colleagues to drink whisky and read his country's illustrated papers (...). For this gradual deterioration of the mind, he held India responsible.

Ho Chi Minh, as a Marxist fighting imperialism more than he was fighting France, the country of Voltaire and Montesquieu, criticized the rapacity of the French. It fed his anger and his resentment.

During the conquest, military operations drove peasants out of their villages. When they returned, they found that their rice paddies had been taken over by franchise holders who had come in the occupation armies' trucks and had not hesitated to divide up among themselves the lands that our farmers had been working for generations. As a result, our peasants became serfs reduced to working their own rice paddies for the benefit of foreign masters. [...]

This despoliation was carried out for franchise holders who had only to say the word to obtain farms that were sometimes larger than 20,000 hectares. Then, after having stolen the fertile land, the French sharks levied taxes on the poor land that were a hundred times more scandalous than the feudal taxes. Oppressed like Annamites, expropriated like peasants, robbed on all sides by the government, the Church, and the missions. The Holy Apostolic Mission alone owns one-ninth of the country's rice paddies.

The person who has most forcefully expressed the discourse of resentment is no doubt Frantz Fanon. He is speaking of Algeria.

The colonist's city is a hard city, all stone and iron. It's a city that is lit and paved, and where the ashbins are full of refuse that is unknown, not even dreamed of. The colonist's feet are never seen, except perhaps at the beach. Feet protected by sturdy shoes, whereas the streets of their city are smooth, without holes or stones.

The colonized person looks on the colonist's city with lust, with desire. Dreams of possession: sitting at the colonist's table, sleeping in his bed, with his wife, if possible. The colonist knows this. 'They want to take our place.' That's true. There is no colonized person who has not dreamed at least once of one day taking the colonist's place.

But for Fanon, in addition to this desire there are also other, more central characteristics.

For the colonized people, the value that is most essential, because it is the most concrete, is the land. The land that is supposed to provide bread and, of course, dignity.

This dignity has nothing to do with the dignity of the human person.

The colonized person has never heard of that ideal human person. What he has seen on his land is that one can arrest him, strike him, starve him with impunity. And never has any teacher of morality, never any priest, never, come to take the blows in his place, or to share his bread with him.

For the colonized person, being moral means, very concretely, silencing the colonist's arrogance, halting his violence, expelling him from the scene.

The violence of this text, compared with the terms used by Nehru and even Ho Chi Minh in criticizing the colonizer, prefigures the tragedies that were to follow, not only terrorism and the war fought against the French but also the rancor and resentment inherited from that period. They led to a civil war which resulted in almost 100,000 deaths during the 1990s.

First of all, let us simply observe that in France, the trauma that arose from four years of foreign occupation still continues to trouble its citizens sixty years later. In Algeria, the natives lived under occupation for more than one hundred and twenty years, while retaining the memory of having been already occupied by foreigners, by the "Roumi" (Romans), the "ancestors" of the French. That is what accounts for a fury that is repressed and still not extinguished.

Moreover, the French and other colonists seized lands, as they did in Vietnam, a despoliation that was much more painful than other actions connected with foreign domination, such as the presence of a government bureaucracy. We see that the resentment felt by the colonized peoples is all the more acute because their land has been taken away or confiscated. And because the countries where the conflicts have been most violent are connected with this despoliation: Algeria, Kenya, Zimbabwe, South Africa, and Israel, where the creation of the state of Israel is perceived by Palestinian Arabs as a colonial conquest. Inversely, in colonies where little land has been seized – in French West Africa – what is called "decolonization" took place with fewer human casualties.

The second fact that accounts for the nature and the degree of resentment with regard to colonialists is the latter's relationship to the identity of the colonized peoples. If the English long showed scorn and indifference toward Hindus, they kept out of their lives,

The Battle of Algiers, or resentment against colonialist violence.

with the exception of Englishmen who took Indian mistresses, a practice that gradually became less frequent because it threatened the men's careers. To avoid taking care of Indians in the event of epidemics, the English trained native doctors, and are not suspected of wanting to proceed with the "anglicizing" of the "natives."

The attitude of the French was different. If, for example, Moroccans still praise Lyautey,[26] that is because he said he respected the country's traditions. In fact, he was thereby stating his conception of the French protectorate. Inversely, he is reproached for having helped perpetuate authoritarian institutions. It remains that he did not seek to overthrow the modes of government that existed in the country. When his successor, Governor Steeg, tried to exempt part of the population – through his decree known as the Berber Dahir – a riot resulted.

It was precisely in Algeria where the French were not able to see that Islam existed without a clergy and that separating religion from politics was not a possibility for the simple reason that alle-

[26] French military governor and then Resident-General of Morocco, 1907–1925.

giance to God is direct and does not pass through anyone. What Muslim law had regulated, secular law destroyed in part. The result was that private life, the household, the wife, constituted "asylums" that were supposed to remain inviolable, so that the identity of the family might be safeguarded. In this context, religion is thus not a matter of conscience or faith; instead, it coincides with certain rules of life. It remains that often uprooted and excluded from the world of the Europeans, without much chance of rising in society, and sensitive to ordinary racism ("Call the witnesses, two men and an Arab"), the "native's" resentment is constantly fed by these attacks on his dignity.

Another grievance fed the resentment of the colonized peoples, notably in Algeria: the colonizers did not keep their promises. Apart from the fact that "native" troops that had fought for France expected to receive, once the war was over, full French citizenship in recognition of their sacrifices, out of 233,000 men, only a handful received that recognition. Above all, the Algerians then saw, between 1947 and 1954, how the French law on the status of Algeria[27] was only an institutional trick that kept the native population from assuming real responsibilities.

The assembly consisted of two houses, one for Europeans and for the few natives whose right to citizenship had been recognized, where electoral procedures functioned normally, and another in which Europeans had as many seats as the natives, who were eight times more numerous in the country. Above all, the fraud practiced in these elections came in addition to a parody of democracy: deceptive ballots, stuffed ballot boxes, and falsification of the results by the authorities were common. This masquerade was called "Naegelen-style elections," after the Socialist governor at that time.

European colonists put pressure on the authorities to perpetuate this situation. Henri Borgeaud, one of the strongmen in the parliamentary world and himself a major colonist, explained that "Algerian political cooking is done in an Algerian kettle, by Algerian cooks. That is, of course, by Europeans living in Algeria." "Honest elections, give us a break, there'll be no political problem if you don't create one," he explained to François Mitterrand's

[27] [Translator's note: Under this law, Algeria was composed of three French "departments" and had a governor named by the French.]

political director, Pierre Nicolai. Here we can discern a certain resentment on the part of Pieds-Noirs (French living in Algeria) against continental France's interference in their affairs. As for the "natives," although they did not have explicit knowledge of what was said by those who in fact controlled Algerian affairs, they were well aware of what was generally thought of them.

When the left came to power in France it let the administration in Algeria continue to fix elections: that was what exasperated the nationalist militants in Algeria, whether they were moderates supporting Ferhat Abbas or radicals supporting Messali. In addition, on the slightest occasion, they were hauled up before the judges as having violated article 80, which concerned attacks on sovereignty: most of the lawyers came from France, but the judges were Europeans living in Algeria. A Republic that didn't keep its word was what destroyed respect for the principles on which it claimed to rely and led to a rehabilitation of the indigenous culture, where keeping one's word and a sense of honor are the foundations of morality. This strengthened nationalist convictions, which during the 1950s were fed by other sources: the rise of the Arab world in the time of Nasser, a return to Islam (to which we shall come back), the example of neighbors, Morocco and Tunisia, which had thrown off the chains of the protectorate.

The resentment against "colonialism" grew stronger and stronger. At home, however, although it was directed against institutions, the regime, and the powerful colonists who embodied it, we see that it did not much concern individuals, even if the native was constantly wounded by the expression of "ordinary racism." On farms as in the city, a certain fraternity of life existed between Europeans and Muslims, despite the double barrier separating them: that of political responsibilities and sexual relations, which were banned in each community. "Two peoples who hate and adore each other," I wrote in *Paris-Normandie* in 1954.

When the militant nationalists, having torn each other to pieces, were brought under the control of the FLN (National Liberation Front) in 1954, there were few individual attacks on Europeans that bore the mark of personal vengeance. Crimes were anonymous and committed by groups that "came from elsewhere," a situation that reappeared forty years later, when Algerians began killing each other again. At the beginning of the Algerian War, when the FLN had not yet gained control of the whole of the population – a control established through terrorism – there were many cases in which natives warned Europeans of the danger threatening them.

Beyond the warfare that was to follow, and its fierceness, this absence of personal resentment accounts for the enthusiasm with which French President Chirac was received in Algeria a few years ago. It shows that the memory of a past that was shared and even happy was returning. For their part, Algerian leaders instrumentalized the resentment that had overwhelmed everything else during the war with France, and which has remained one of the foundations of their legitimacy.

The Pieds-Noirs were angry with the continental French for not having been able to defend them. Above all, they felt betrayed by de Gaulle, whom they had trusted when they launched a coup d'etat on 13 May 1958. "We will never be anti-Gaullist enough," said those who saw the meaning of the small steps that de Gaulle was making in a direction contrary to the one the Pieds-Noirs wanted to pursue. Although he probably thought that independence might be the outcome of his actions, and that, given the state of the insurrection, there was no possibility of returning to "papa's Algeria," he did not imagine that the insurrection would lead to the departure of all the French, an exodus for which they have never pardoned him.

Nonetheless, in continental France as in Algeria, after the latter gained independence there were French people who thought it would be possible to cooperate with the new leaders. Some had supported the Algerian cause, had condemned torture and shown "more compassion for its victims than for those of terrorism," as Jacques Soustelle and Albert Camus said. The would-be cooperators intended to treat independent Algerians the way French leaders ought to have treated them during the time when Algeria consisted of three French departments. Even though they were not suspect of harboring colonial ideas, they became disenchanted as soon as they were no longer dealing with leaders shaped by the principles of Western democracies, as Benkedda, Ferhat Abbas, and Ait Ahmed were, but with Ben Bella, and especially Boumediene, who, basing himself on the army and traditional society, sought to promote Islam and to de-Gallicize the country the better to Arabize it. The resentment of these

French people who were disappointed by the turn taken by the Algerian government was soon accompanied by that of Algerian women who had thought independence would bring them freedom.

When France controlled Algeria, Muslim families resisted Europeanization in order to defend their identity. It was often the respect for traditions that counted, religion being less a matter of conscience than an identification with certain rules of life. The family being the "fortress" that colonization had not penetrated, girls were not sent to European schools: in the lycée Stéphane-Gsell in Oran, for instance, between 1948 and 1956 there were fewer than ten girls whose parents allowed them to continue their studies as far as the baccalaureate.

During the struggle for liberation, the FLN had talked about women's future and their emancipation once Algeria had won its independence. Many women participated in the fighting, essentially out of patriotism, but also because they believed this promise of emancipation. But the changes that took place in the state leadership between 1961 and 1965, along with a movement from the depths of society, put an end to that hope. In her film *La Nouba des femmes du mont Chenoua*, one of the first of these women, Assia Djebar, powerfully expressed her disillusionment and her anger at being once again relegated and at these unkept promises. During the 1970s, women protested and demonstrated; they were harshly repressed. In 1984, Algerian leaders gave Islamists a pledge by adopting a personal status law modeled on Sharia.

Islam's revival of resentment

The resentment that the native peoples of Algeria showed against the colonizer resembled that of colonized peoples in India, Indonesia, and Vietnam. However, in the worlds of Islam, it was rooted in a humiliation deeper than elsewhere because in the past Islam had dominated the peoples who had now colonized them. "How could we become the slaves of those who were our slaves?" That is the question asked by those who know that in 1830 there were Christian slaves in Algiers, and in 1880 Caucasian slaves in Cairo. More generally, Muslims remember the time when empires inherited from the Arab conquest dominated both the West and the East: the Ottomans, from Morocco to Crimea, the Persian

Safavids, from the Caspian to the Indus, and the Moghuls, from Kashmir to the Bay of Bengal.

The Moghul Empire, however, disappeared in the eighteenth century: in 1907 British and Russian "spheres of influence" were imposed on the Persian Empire, and the Ottoman Empire was defeated in 1918 and then destroyed, after having been divided up by the Europeans and seeing its Christian minorities become independent (Greece, Bulgaria, and others).

The end of the Ottoman Empire was accompanied by the suppression of the Caliphate, which was then represented by the Sultan, who incarnated the line of Muhammad and the unity of Islam (except for the Shi'ites). This suppression was carried out by Kemal Atatürk, who wanted to modernize the Turkish world by secularizing it. Though Atatürk was not anti-religious, his action nonetheless was seen as sacrilegious, and in 1928 the Muslim Brotherhood was founded in Cairo to oppose this modernization.

Moreover, we can now see that the strongest reactions against the humiliation produced by colonization, or against the subversion produced by modernity, emerged from individuals or groups that came from areas that were the least "contaminated" by European expansion: Egypt, first of all; then Khomeini's Iran in 1979, Afghanistan and its Pashtun areas, Yemen, and the Arabian peninsula, where Wahhabism, a fundamentalist movement that urges a return to Sharia, appeared in the eighteenth century.

In 2001, when Bin Laden explained the attacks on the World Trade Center and the Pentagon, he referred to "eighty years of humiliation of Muslim peoples," a precise allusion to Atatürk's suppression of the Caliphate. But he said nothing about the contemporaneous birth of Arab states, because nation-states – that "Western invention" – are a factor in the division of Islam. This also accounts for the Muslim Brotherhood's hostility to them. And it also explains why Bin Laden, though he supports the Palestinians against Israel, never supported Yasser Arafat, who divided the Arab-Muslim East even further by trying to create a new state; moreover, Arafat incarnated a certain kind of secularism; he did not mention Islam even once when he spoke before the United Nations Assembly in 1974.

An illustration that appeared in the children's magazine *Al-da'Wa* in 1978, and was reproduced in the French *Choc de l'Islam*, sums up all the grievances of militant Islam. An enormous finger points at the greatest of Islam's enemies, Theodor Herzl, one of the founders of Zionism. Those who supported him are represented in little vignettes: Assad, the leader of the secular Ba'ath party in Syria; Brezhnev, the incarnation of atheistic Communism; Begin, who was then prime minister of Israel; Nasser, who was guilty of having strengthened the nation-state; the Star of David, the Statue of Liberty, the hammer and sickle, and finally, Kemal Atatürk, the herald of secularism in the Islamic world.

But all this does not explain another frustration: the failure of these nation-states to carry out the economic modernization that was supposed to be permitted by gaining independence. Although this promise was telescoped by the acceleration of globalization, internal political dysfunctions and rivalries compromised the rise of these countries.

The shah's Iran and Boumediene's Algeria did not lack natural resources, especially oil. The brutality of the steps taken by the state to equip the country, on the one hand, and misappropriation of funds and corruption on the other, have deprived the people of the dividends from this manna, driving them toward extreme forms of Islam, whether Shi'ite or Sunni. American intervention has moreover played the role of a trigger in Shi'ite Iran and in the opposition in Sunni Saudi Arabia. Other, less well endowed countries that still have a rich agricultural and cultural tradition have been affected by the same phenomenon: Egypt, where the Muslim Brotherhood has taken over many areas of the state, and Morocco, where the class divisions perpetuate those of the colonial period, and the practices of the government, if not its legitimacy, are contested.

The resentment against the perverse effects of globalization and the conviction that it is the United States that controls what happens add to the paralysis of the modernist transformation that the people expected at the time independence was won. The observation that the countries of the Far East, which were also once colonized, have been able to graft themselves onto the developing world and not remain frozen in rejection – that is what challenges the dogma and the law of Islam. Islam's responsibility can only deepen the schism within its highly diverse societies. Isn't the clash of civilizations located within Islam as much as it is in its relationships with others?

Communalism and revolution

In the countries of the Maghreb, and especially in Algeria, the colonial heritage, the disillusions of independence, and the cruellest kind of civil war have resulted in whole population groups continuing to emigrate to France. The total number of these Maghrebin immigrants has been estimated at three to five million, depending on whether one counts such as those who have been naturalized or temporary immigrants. I refer to "Maghrebin immigrants" and not to "Muslims" because it seems unjustified to consider as Islamic a population that goes to mosques even less frequently than French Catholics go to church. But – and we shall return to this later on – every time there is a problem with these immigrants, the Interior minister is called upon to settle them, and he deals with the representatives of Islam ...

"I was expecting that it would be the left that appointed me a state secretary, and to my great surprise it was the right." Making this remark when Jean-Pierre Raffarin brought her into his government in 2004, Tokia Saifi broke a kind of taboo by drawing attention to the fact that since 1981 no socialist government had appointed an immigrant from the Maghreb to high state office. It is easy to understand why immigrants from North Africa who are Muslims have felt some bitterness. All the more, because the French left – and not only the socialists – has constantly asserted its anti-racism and participated in the battles fought by SOS-Racisme. But this left "has never brought them into its house."

In addition, with respect to its revolutionary discourse, the left has always looked with favor on the most extreme among these immigrants. This is nothing new. Before the Algerian war, at a time when the left wing of the left was represented by the Communists, the latter preferred to deal with Messali Hadj, who was, of course, a supporter of independence and a nationalist, but who always spoke up for Islam, rather than with Ferhat Abbas, a secular Muslim who represented the bourgeoisie, "a class without a future." After independence, the far left, now Trotskyist, considered anything better in continental France than the Republican nation-state. Around 1968, the Trotskyists once again had faith in worldwide revolution and sided with those who could guarantee its future: Fidel Castro, Yasser Arafat, and Boumediene. The Maoists soon joined the movement.

None of them knew much about or respected immigrants who wanted to become French. Some of these immigrants were considered traitors because they had not fought for the independence of their country. Such battles weakened the imperialist or bourgeois world, and Lenin had already said that anything that moved in the direction of revolution was moral, and anything that opposed it was immoral.

During the 1970s – the period when Pompidou and Giscard d'Estaing headed the French government – the far left understood that the worldwide revolution was not taking place because the "bourgeoisie" (for them, this meant the state) had taken power once again. As a result the Trotskyists, with the Lambertists in the van, and Maoists as well, converted and dissolved in order to engage in "entrism"[28] in political parties, trade unions, the state apparatus, and the press. Ecology was used by many of them as a backup structure.

They were most numerous in the Socialist Party: at the Socialist left's congress in 1994, Gérard Filoche tells us, out of 500 delegates there were 180 former members of the *Ligue communiste*, ten former Lambertists, and three former members of *Lutte ouvrière*. In this context, a survival of their repressed past, they could not imagine calling for the support of the *beurs* (second-generation North African immigrants) who had wanted to trust the Republican state. These *beurs*, who were victims of ordinary racism and unlike their forebears expressed their anger in French, saw that "the housing project is not the site of their citizenship but that of its denial."[29] In Algeria, their fathers told the French left: "You claim to be our brothers, but we want to be your brothers-in-law." In France, the *beurs* have become brothers-in-law of the French, as is shown by the growing number of mixed marriages, but politically they are still excluded.

Then, to show their good will – applying to politics the principle of precaution, so much does Islamism threaten the heart of Europe – our leaders, on the left and on the right, Islamize the Maghrebins. They make Muslim organizations their "valid inter-

---

[28] The "Lambertist" group, which appeared in 1955, specialized in taking over political and trade union organisms, and then the media, by means of "entrism," that is, joining a group without flying its flag.
[29] Gilles Kepel.

locutors," strengthen them, as they did during the Algerian war, when they sought them out among the nationalist organizations. Or as was done during the Revolution and the Napoleonic period, when religions were created the better to control the servants. Except that these same leaders did not realize that alongside the hard-core Muslims, the second- and third-generation Maghrebins practiced their religion less and less. And that the defense of identity-related rights remains a safeguard for use when they have no other. Consequently, some people think that not respecting these rights – for example, regarding wearing the Islamic veil – is equivalent to not respecting the right to be different. And they attack integration, which they see as a relic of colonialism. Whereas in colonial times the natives reproached the home country and the colonists for not making them full citizens. So anti-racism has become a defense of the right to differentiate oneself from others. If immigrants are victims, the galaxy of far-left organizations can conclude that the immigrants' sense of belonging to a community could substitute for what was once, for the working class, class consciousness. And these immigrants would thus have a revolutionary role to play.

The Communists were thrown into great confusion when first the working class partly deserted them, while at the same time its original numbers in France declined, and then the collapse of the USSR had the devastating effect of undermining all the foundations of revolutionary ideology: state control of the economy, the party's colonization of social institutions, and so on. Above all, the USSR had lost its function as a "fortress" which, though corrupt, it continued to play, limiting the liberal bourgeoisie's ability to ignore popular demands, and thus guaranteeing the extension of the welfare state.

The resentment of revolutionary militants against the Soviet regime and its heirs that "have betrayed world revolution at the time of Stalin and then abandoned workers to their fate all over the world" – that resentment is truly unlimited. Moreover, their hatred of Putin is twice as great, because he has restored a free economy, adding to the humiliation of those who believed only in a planned economy. At least they could condemn with good conscience Russian policy in Chechnya, the Chechens being, as the Algerians had been, the victims of a new kind of imperialism. So that today in France, in the spirit of the far left, ethnic communalism might play the same role that used to be played, for the Communist Party, by a proletariat, which constituted a counter-society. By substituting for the latter, ethnic communalism is supposed to operate as a revolutionary lever under two conditions:

- that immigration increase, which would show that anti-racism has been converted into "immigrations," and
- that this communalism be more or less associated with Islamism, a real and effective enemy of imperialism.

At the time of the Islamic Revolution in 1979, Michel Foucault succumbed to the temptation to hail its purity. Others have since invoked the American model to legitimate this communalism, from which a form of multiculturalism might emerge. This is to forget that in the United States communalism is patriotic: each group tries to be more patriotic than the others, whereas in France Islamist communities behave like foreigners.

It is certain that in France the instrumentalization of communalism for revolutionary ends is based on an illusion. Even if Islamist leaders dominate their own community (and French policy has helped them do so) before imposing their law on the rest of non-Muslim society – in schools, hospitals, for instance – we can bet that most Maghrebins – and this is a difference from the situation twenty years ago, when they were less integrated – will end up adopting the rules of secularism provided that they are applied fairly, rather than return to Sharia or participate in revolutionary adventures. These two resentments that have lived together – are they going to live apart?

5

Conclusion

In "L'Histoire anonyme" I tried to determine the spectrum of the behavior of simple individuals like you and me when faced with an economic crisis, a war, or a revolution. Resentment, a few historical manifestations of which I have analyzed here, whether individual or collective, arises from a humiliation or a trauma that may be caused by social extraction, by physical weakness – Gandhi acknowledges how much the vigor of the English aroused Indians' admiration and envy – and more generally, by an inferiority complex. Exceptional circumstances can crystallize resentment, act as a trigger, but they are not necessary for the "man of resentment" to show his suffering.

In his *Notes from the Underground*, Dostoyevsky has admirably described this "man of resentment." A century later, Albert Camus, a teenager, a little white boy, a very little white boy at the bottom of the social ladder with a handicapped uncle, a quasi-illiterate mother, and himself a ward of the state, could not have failed to feel these humiliations before he became *l'homme révolté* (*The Rebel*, the title of one of Camus' books). He was almost at the level of the Arabs. He was politically active, became a Communist, in order to win recognition of Arabs' rights. Like that of several revolutionaries in 1789 and 1917, Camus' case provides an example of the bonds that can be forged between an individual's resentment and that of a collectivity. How one can come to represent and express the other. Internalized, the suffering of these

men and women gnaws at them like a cancer. The resentment it
can produce is the precursor of revolt. Resentment, revolt, revolution, the return of a wound from the past, makes it more
present than the present. It distorts history's relation to time, a
problem that François Hartog has studied.

The forms taken by these re-actions have characteristics that
the analysis of societies allows us to identify. First of all, resentment is not necessarily associated with a specific demand. Naturally, the latter may accompany it, but the examples of 1789 and
1917 show that satisfying this demand does not suffice to do away
with resentment. That is because the long impotence of those who
have felt themselves to be the victims of humiliations has increased
their aggressiveness. In 2001, the resentment expressed by Al-
Qaeda toward the Western world was not accompanied by any
demand, as if to prevent its adversaries from understanding the
acts that its networks might commit. Therein resides one of the
differences between the actions of this Islamist group and those
of Palestinian terrorist groups, whose objective is well-defined:
nothing less than the destruction of the State of Israel.

In history, resentment has been the matrix of ideologies of
protest, on the left and on the right. The frustrations that produce
it – broken promises, disillusionments, and wounds – provoke an
impotent anger that lends it substance. Suffering caused by being
poor, excluded, or the fear of becoming poor and excluded, have
fed numerous social movements whose characteristics were not
determined in advance. "Yes, people have to understand that men
mutilated in the war do not consider themselves pariahs," Maurice
Leblanc wrote shortly after the First World War. "What? You
think that just because they have been amputated, men who used
their legs to run to attack are going to be outdistanced by people
who warmed their feet at the fire in an office? Get out of our way!
We know how to take this place."

All of these men, whether amputated or not, experienced the
bitterness of a difficult readaptation to civilian life. Cleverly flat-
tering these veterans, governments did not guarantee to fulfill the
claims they had on the nation. Because governments did not organize the veterans' return to civilian life, the latter were condemned
to be unemployed. The discourse of the leaders made their lack
of interest all the more odious to these wretched men. The old
wounds that had just healed were opened up again: resentment

against the men who had had cushy positions, the bitter memory of furloughs, and the real or supposed misconduct of wives all welded these veterans together in opposition to the people who stayed behind the lines. But later on, were these unemployed protestors who marched through London in 1919 wearing their berets going to join the Labour Party or Mosley's Fascist troops? In any event, one thing was sure: they ridiculed those who repeated that the veterans had been the dupes of big capital and the arms merchants, who were supposed to have manipulated them like marionettes. This denigration added to their humiliation and drove them to close ranks, to justify their sacrifice, and to share nationalist ideas.

If the bond that can be forged between individual resentment and collective resentment is indeed one of the characteristics that this investigation has revealed, along with the ambivalence of the sign of revolt that resentment can produce, another observation also has to be made that did not figure among our initial hypotheses: *resentment is reciprocal*. Resentment is not peculiar to those whom we identified at the outset as victims: slaves, oppressed classes, defeated peoples, and so on. Our inquiry has shown that resentment can strike simultaneously or in alternation not just one of the parties involved, but both. An obvious case of this is a reaction that follows a revolution, but developments of this kind are multiple and diverse. At the beginnings of Christianity, the Church, once it had been made official, passed from being persecuted to being a persecutor, notably of heretics. At the other extremity of history, the Nazis' resentment against the Jews, who were supposed to be preventing Germany from realizing its destiny, corresponds to the survivors' resentment. After the war, there were Germans who "pardoned" Jews for their imaginary crimes, and who aroused in some people, like Jean Amery, the resentment they wanted to end.

There are places where this reciprocity, whether synchronous or alternating, is preserved. We owe the identification of these "realms of memory" to Pierre Nora, whether they are schools, the Catholic Church, commemorations, or celebrations. But festivals innocently perpetuate resentment, whether in the form of *Moros y Cristianos* in Western Spain, the Passion relived every year in Oberammergau, or the Passion disturbed by Jewish devils in San Fratello in Sicily. It goes without saying that some interpretations of history, of which I have given examples, cause resentments to persist. Nonetheless, the historians' community, thanks to the many colloquia it organizes, has helped defuse many grievances: between Turks and Armenians, between the Chileans and their neighbours, and in the past, between the French and the Germans. It has proven that it has therapeutic virtues insofar as it is not associated with state policies.

The relationships between Catholics and Protestants, even when calmed, attest to the persistence and reciprocity of resentments. This is still shown today by the conventional terms "papists" and *parpaillotes* (Protestants). However, this reciprocity is not a constant. Consider the resentment of the humiliated peasantry studied by Jacques Le Goff. Le Goff noticed that in the West the peasant does not appear in literature for almost eight centuries. Through its Greco-Roman heritage, the society of the high Middle Ages took pride in idleness in a world that lived off the labor of slaves. As for the Judeo-Christian heritage, it emphasized the primacy of the contemplative life. According to the Rule of St Benedict, manual labour is a form of penitence. Not until the twelfth century did the Church canonize a peasant. These *rustici* are drunk, sick, lustful. Do they even have a name? They are foils who are burdened with an excessively heavy heritage, and continue to bear its stigmata when they are freed, "vilains" who are always dangerous and illiterate. In time, does the peasant internalize the characteristics he has been given? His resentment feeds on them, and he hides the violence society suspects. Unless he avows it and it explodes.

These cases testify to the necessity of taking a long view of social and political history. They remind us how right Fernand Braudel was to question the division of the past into chronological phases. Entirely horizontal, the latter do not allow us to account for the thickness and depth of problems. Incriminating others and promoting oneself is one of the characteristics of resentment. Those who consider themselves victims consider their status undeserved, hence others are to blame for it. The latter's domination and strength are illegitimate, so evident are their duplicity and immorality. Whether it is a matter of the victors of 1918 who applied the principle of the right of self-determination only to their own advantage. Or a matter of France, which called in 1830 for the independence of Belgium and Greece while at the same time seizing Algeria. Or a matter of defending freedom today – that of Rushdie, for instance, whom the mullahs condemn, though this does not prevent the West from signing new commercial treaties with Iran. These hypocrisies deprive these nation-states of any right to brandish their colours and claim to be defending human rights.

In return, the peoples of resentment valorize their own identity. Whether it is a matter of Christians who originally substituted a morality of kindness and charity for a religion of ritual. They also defend a life purified of all the excesses of the flesh and stigmatize, like today's Muslim fundamentalists, the decadence of mores and the excess of pleasures. Or a matter of the Jews, who were for a long time victims of segregation, which they resent as an injustice, whereas they valorize their own past. They congratulate them-selves on having been able to preserve their beliefs and culture despite twenty centuries of persecution. From this ordeal, and from their resentment, arose the Zionist project of re-establishing a state in the Holy Land.

Among American blacks, who are the descendants of slaves, resentment has produced, in addition to revolt, the redemptive conviction that "black is beautiful." And that African civiliza-tions have contributed just as much as others to the human patrimony.

Identity claims thus constitute one of the forms taken by resent-ment when egalitarian utopias have failed. But do they disappear as soon as a strong identity is established? The past century has not provided proof that they will.

Does that mean that the cycle of resentments never ends? That one can never escape being subjected to it?

Provided that the movement is reciprocal, history teaches instead that such claims may fade and no longer be expressed in fits of mad fury. In every case, the forms of political democracy, both direct and representative, and participatory as well, such as exist in northern Europe, attenuate the violence of collective movements even if they do not extirpate individual resentments. Judicial practices can contribute to this, unless they deflect the parties' grievances and impose on them their own habits, thus disguising the frustrations.

The will to eliminate these jolts and excesses has, however, won some magnificent victories. In South Africa, the magnanimity of the parties involved, thanks to the intercession of the Church and women's associations, has made it possible to freeze three-century-old grievances and to master resentments. This example has been more or less followed elsewhere, notably in Peru, where a "peace and reconciliation" commission seems to have put an end to the excesses committed by the opposing parties by appealing to outside institutions such as NGOs. Nonetheless, it is certain that on the one hand, the disillusionment regarding the great hopes raised by the idea of progress, whose promises have not been kept, and on the other hand the tightening of the constraints imposed by the developments of globalization, cannot help but multiply centers of resentment, as the experience of the past century has amply demonstrated. Unless bursts of magnanimity spread, our future does not look bright.

Bibliography

Agulhon, Maurice. *Les Quarante-Huitards*. Paris: Archives Gallimard, 1975.

Allemagne nazie et le génocide juif. Ed. François Furet and Raymond Aron. Paris: Hautes Etudes-Gallimard-Seuil, 1983.

Amery, Jean. *Par-delà le crime et le châtiment*. Paris: Babel, 1995.

"Ancien régime et révolution: interprétation." Introduction by François Furet; articles by Le Roy Ladurie, Bien, Vovelle, Andrews. *Annales, ESe*, 1, pp. 1–139, 1974.

Anders, Wladyslaw. *Mémoires (1939–1946)*. Paris: La Jeune Parque, 1948.

Angenot, Marc. *Les Idéologies du ressentiment*. Montreal: XYZ, 1996.

Archives clandestines du ghetto de Varsovie. Ed. Emmanuel Ringel. Paris: Fayard-BDIC, 2 vols.

Bacharan, Nicole. *Histoire des Noirs américains au XX siècle*. Paris: Complexe, 1994.

Baldwin, James, *et al. The Negro Protest*. Boston: Beacon, 1963.

Baslez, Marie-Françoise. *Les Persécutions dans l' Antiquité, victimes, héros, martyrs*. Paris: Fayard, 2007.

Beauvois, Daniel. *Histoire de la Pologne*. Paris: Hatier, 1995.

Benjamin, Walter. "Theses on the philosophy of history." In *Illuminations*, trans. H. Zohn. New York: Schocken, 1969, pp. 253–64.

Bensoussan, Georges. *Une histoire intellectuelle et politique du sionisme, 1860–1940*. Paris: Fayard, 2001.

Beranger, Jean. *Histoire de l'Empire des Habsbourg*. Paris: Fayard, 1990.

Berce, Yves-Marie. *Croquants et Nu-Pieds*. Paris: Archives, 1974.

Besançon, Alain. "Dostoievski." In *Personnages et caractères*, ed. E. Le Roy Ladurie. Paris: PUF, 2004.

Blanchard, P., N. Bancel, and S. Lemaire. *La Fracture coloniale, la société française au prisme de l'héritage colonial*. Paris: La Découverte, 2005.

Bluche, Frédéric et Stéphane RIALS. *Les Révolutions françaises*. Paris: Fayard, 1989 (especially the articles by Bluche, Rials, Antonetti).

Boureau, Alain. "L'inceste de Judas, essai sur la genèse de la haine antisémite au XIIe siècle." *Penser, rêver, Revue de psychanalyse, 7. Retours sur la question juive*, printemps 2005.

Brown, Peter. *Power and Persuasion in Late Antiquity. Towards a Christian Empire*. Madison: University of Wisconsin Press, 1992.

Burgat, François. *L'Islamisme en face*. Paris: La Découverte, 2002.

Burrin, Philippe. *Hitler et les Juifs, Genèse d'un génocide*. Paris: Seuil, 1989.

Burrin, Philippe. *Ressentiment et apocalypse. Essai sur l'antisémitisme nazi*. Paris: Seuil, 2004.

Camara, Laye. *Le Maître de la parole*. Paris: Plon, 1978.

Carrere d'Encausse, Hélène. *Le Grand Frère*. Paris: Flammarion, 1982.

Chartier, Roger. *Les Origines culturelles de la Révolution française*. Paris: Seuil, 2000.

Cinnella, Ettore. "État 'prolétarien' et science 'bourgeoise': les *spets* pendant les premières années du pouvoir soviétique." *Cahiers du monde russe et soviétique*, 1991, vol. 32, no. 4, pp. 469–501.

Clark, Kenneth. *Ghetto noir*. Preface by G. Myrdal. Paris: Payot, 1966.

Clavreul, Jean. *Le Désir et la loi*. Paris: Denoël, 1987 (ch. 3, on the *Merchant of Venice*), pp. 115–141.

"Color and Race." *Daedalus*, Spring 1967. Especially the articles by Philip Mason and Edward Shils.

Cooley, John. *Unholy Wars, Afghanistan, America and International Terrorism*. London: Pluto Press, 1999.

Cottias, Myriam. "L'oubli du passé contre la citoyenneté: troc et ressentiment à la Martinique (1848–1946)." In Fred Constant and Justin Daniel, *1946–1996, Cinquante Ans de départementalisation outre-mer*. Paris: L'Harmattan, 1997, pp. 293–313.

Courtois, Stéphane (ed.) *Une si longue nuit, l'apogée des régimes totalitaires*. Monaco: Éditions du Rocher, 2003. Especially Andrzej Packowski's article on Poland.

Cranshaw, Edward. *La Chute des Habsbourg*. Paris: Gallimard, 1963.

Crouzet, François. *De la supériorité de l'Angleterre sur la France, l'économique et l'imaginaire*. Preface by Pierre Chaunu. Paris: Perrin, 1999.

Daix, Pierre. *La Crise du PCF*. Paris: Seuil, 1968.

Davies, Norman. *God's Playground. A History of Poland.* Oxford: Oxford University Press, 1982.

Dieckhoff, Alain, and Kastoryano Riva. *Nationalismes en mutation en Méditerranée orientale.* Paris: CNRS, 2007.

Dostoyevsky, Feodor. *Notes from Underground.* Trans. M. R. Katz. New York: Norton, 1989.

Doyle, William. *Des origines à la Révolution française.* Paris: Calmann-Lévy, 1988.

Duchet, Claude and Patrice de Comarmond, eds. *Racisme et société.* Paris: Maspero, 1969.

Durandin, Cathérine. *Révolution à la française ou à la russe.* Paris: PUF, 1989.

Ertel, Rachel. *Le Shtetl, la bourgade juive en Pologne.* Paris: Payot, 1982.

"Êtes-vous ressentimental?" In *La Célibataire, revue de psychanalyse,* 5, été-automne 2001. Especially the articles by Charles Melman, Cyril Veken, Helene L'Heuillet.

Favret-Saada, Jeanne, in collaboration with Josée Contreras. *Le Christianisme et ses Juifs, 1800–2000.* Paris: Seuil, 2004.

Ferro, Marc. *Histoire de France.* Paris: Odile Jacob, 2001–2003.

Ferro, Marc. *Le Choc de !'Islam.* Paris: Odile Jacob, 2002.

Ferro, Marc. *Les Origines de la perestroika.* Paris: Ramsay, 1990.

Ferry, Luc. *Apprendre à vivre.* Paris: Plon, 2006.

Fitzpatrick, Sheila. "The Bolshevik dilemma: class, culture and politics in the early soviet years." *Slavic Review,* 1988, vol. 47, no. 4.

Fromm, Erich. *La Peur de la liberté.* Paris: Buchet-Chastel, 1963.

Furet, François and Mona Ozouf. *Dictionnaire critique de la Révolution française.* Paris: Flammarion, 1988. See especially, in addition to the articles by Furet and Ozouf, those by Bronislaw Baczko, David D. Bien, Patrice Gueniffey, Marcel Gauchet, Ran Halevy.

Gauchet, Marcel. *La Condition historique. Entretiens avec François Azouvi et Sylvain Piron.* Paris: Stock, 2003.

Green, Nancy L. "Juifs et Noirs aux Etats-Unis, la rupture d'une alliance naturelle." In *Annales ESC,* 2, pp. 445–65, 1987.

Gross, Jan T. *Les voisins, 10 juillet 1941, un massacre de Juifs en Pologne.* Paris: Fayard, 2002.

Gurjanov, Alexander. "Soviet repressions towards Poles and Polish citizens in 1936–1956 in the light of soviet documents." *Europa Nie prowincjonalna,* ed. Krysztofa Jasiewicza. Warsaw and London, 2000.

Hamann, Brigitte. *Hitler's Vienna: A Dictator's Apprenticeship.* Oxford: Oxford University Press, 1999.

Hartog, François. *Régimes d'historicité, présentisme et expérience du temps.* Paris: Seuil, 2003.

Hegel, G. W. F. *L'Esprit du christianisme et son destin*, précéde de *L'Esprit du judaïsme* (1795–1799). Paris: Vrin, 2003.

Hirsh, Jean-Pierre. *La Nuit du 4 août.* Paris: Archives Gallimard, 1978.

Honour and Shame, the values of Mediterranean society. Ed. J. G. Peristiany. London: Weidenfeld and Nicolson, 1966 (especially the article by Caro Baroja), 1965.

Identités de l'Europe centrale. Ed. Michael Maslowski. Paris: Institut d'études slaves, 1996.

Jacquard, Roland and Tazaghart Atmane. *Bin Laden, la destruction programmée de l'Occident.* Paris: Jean Picollec, 2004.

Jeismann, Michael. *La Patrie de l'ennemi, la notion d'ennemi national et la représentation en Allemagne et en France de 1792 à 1918.* Paris: CNRS, 1997.

Jordan, June. *Afro-American Poetry.* New York: Zenith, 1970.

Schnapp, Alain and Pierre Vidal-Naquet. *Journal de la commune étudiante, Textes et documents, sept. 1967, juin 1968.* Paris: Seuil, 1969.

Kaplan, Lawrence, ed. *Revolutions, a Comparative Study.* New York: Random House, 1973.

Kende, P., and K. Pomian. *Varsovie-Budapest, 1956.* Paris: Seuil, 1978.

Kepel, Gilles. *Jihad, Expansion et déclin de l'islamisme.* Paris: Gallimard, 2000.

Kershaw, Ian. *The Nazi dictatorship: problems and perspectives of interpretation.* London: Arnold, 4th edn 2000.

Klyuchevsky, Vasilii. *A History of Russia*, 5 vols. London: 1955.

Kriegel Maurice, «Les Juifs», *in* Le Goff-Schmitt, pp. 569–587.

Laborie, Pierre. *Les Français des années troubles.* Paris: Desclée de Brouwer, 2001.

Langmuir, G. "L'absence d'accusation de meurtre rituel à l'ouest du Rhône." In *Juifs et Judaïsme en Languedoc, Cahiers de Fanjeaux.* Paris: Privat, 1977.

Laurens, Henri. *La Question de la Palestine*, 2 vols. Paris: Fayard, 1999 and 2002.

Le Goff, Jacques and Jean-Claude Schmitt. *Dictionnaire raisonné de l'Occident médiéval.* Paris: Fayard, 1999.

Lefranc, Georges. *Le Mouvement socialiste sous la IIIe République, (1875–1940).* Paris: Payot, 1963.

Lepelley, Claude. *L'Empire romain et le christianisme.* Paris: Flammarion, 1969.

Levesque, Jacques. *1989, la fin d'un Empire, l'URSS et la libération de l'Europe de l'Est.* Paris: Presses de la FNSP, 1995.

Lewis, Bernard. *Le Retour de l'Islam*, Gallimard, 1985.

Lewis, Bernard. *Race and Color in Islam*. New York: Harper and Row, 1971.

Martinez-Gras, Gabriel and Lucette Valensi. *L'Islam en dissidence, genèse d'un affrontement*. Paris: Seuil, 2004.

Meddeb, Adelwahab. *La Maladie de l'Islam*. Paris: Seuil, 2002.

Mele, Giannarita. "Théorie et organisation des pratiques culturelles à l'époque du Proletkult." In Ferro and Fitzpatrick, *Culture et Révolution*. Paris: EHESS, 1989, pp. 41–71.

Mommsen, Hans. *Le national-socialisme et la société allemande*. Preface by H. Rousso. Paris: Éditions de la MSH, 1997.

Moscovici, Serge, "Le ressentiment, suivi d'extraits d'interviews." *Le Genre humain*, automne-hiver 1984–1985, pp. 179–206.

Murray, Frame, "Censorship and control in the Russian Imperial theatres during the 1905 revolution and its aftermath." *Revolutionary Russia*, vol. 7, Dec. 1994, pp. 164–192.

Ngoupande, Jean-Paul. *L'Afrique face à l'Islam*. Paris: Albin Michel, 2003.

Nicolas, Jean. *La Rébellion française – Mouvements populaires et conscience sociale, 1661–1789*. Paris: Seuil, 2005.

Nietzsche, Friedrich, *The Gay Science* (1882). Trans. W. Kaufmann. New York: Random House, 1974.

Nietzsche, Friedrich. *The Genealogy of Morals*. Trans. W. Kaufmann. New York: Vintage, 1984.

Nolte, Ernst, *Les Mouvements fascistes, l'Europe de 1919 à 1945*. Preface by Alain Renaut. Paris: Calmann-Lévy, 1969; rpt. Hachette, 1992.

Notin, Jean-Christophe. *La Campagne d'Italie. Les victoires oubliées de la France (1943–1945)*. Paris: Perrin, 2002.

Ory, Pascal. *La France allemande (1933–1945). Paroles de collaborationnisme*. Paris: Archives-Gallimard, 1977.

Peristiany, J. G. and Julian Pitt-Rivers. *Honor and Grace in Anthropology*. Cambridge: Cambridge University Press, 1992.

Petre-Grenouilleau, Olivier, *Les Traites negrières*. Paris: Gallimard, 2004.

Piganiol, André. *L'Empire chrétien*. Paris: PUF, 1944.

Poliakov, Léon. *Le Mythe aryen*. Paris: Calmann-Lévy, 1971.

Poliakov, Léon, *Histoire de l'antisémitisme*. Paris: Calmann-Lévy, 3 vols., 1968.

Pomian, Krzysztof. *Pologne, défi à l'impossible: de la révolte de Poznan à Solidarité*. Paris: Éditions Ouvrières, 1982.

Popovitch, Alexandre. "La Révolte des Zandj." *Cahiers de la Méditerranée*, vol. 65.

Popovitch, Alexandre. *La Révolte des Zandj*. Paris: EHESS, 1976.

Rawls, John. *A Theory of Justice*. Oxford: Clarendon, 1972, pp. 530–41, 1971.

Rebillard, Eric. "La conversion de l' Empire romain selon Peter Brown." In *Annales, HSS*, 4, pp. 813–23, 1999.

Reimann, Viktor. *Joseph Goebbels*. Paris: Flammarion, 1973.

Rene-Chardavoine, Monique. *La Croisade albigeoise*. Paris: Archives Gallimard, 1979.

Révolte et société. Presented by Philippe JANSEN, 2 vols, Paris: Sorbonne, "Histoire au présent," 1989. Especially the articles by A. de Baecke and Rémy Puech.

Rovan, Joseph. *Histoire de l'Allemagne*. Paris: Seuil, 1999.

Rowan, Carl T. *Just between us Blacks*. New York: Random House, 1974.

Roy, Olivier. *L'Echec de l'Islam politique*. Paris: Seuil, 1992.

Rupnik, Jacques. *L'Autre Europe, Crise et fin du communisme*. Paris: Odile Jacob, 1990.

Scheler, Max. *Das Ressentiment im Aufbau der Moralen* (1912). English trans., *Ressentiment*, edited by Lewis A. Coser, translated by William W. Holdheim. New York: Schocken. 1972. French trans., *L'Homme du ressentiment*. Paris: Gallimard, 1933.

Scheler, Max. *Zur Phänomenologie und Theorie der Sympathiegefühle und von Liebe und Haß*, 1913; reissued as *Wesen und Formen der Sympathie*, 1923. French trans. *Le Sens de la souffrance*. Paris: Gallimard, 1945.

Scherrer, Jutta. "Pour l'hégémonie culturelle du prolétariat: aux origines du concept de culture prolétarienne." In M. Ferro and S. Fitzpatrick, *Culture et Révolution*. Paris: EHESS, 1989, pp. 11–25.

Schorske, Carl E. *Fin de siècle Vienna: Politics and Culture*. New York: Knopf, 1979.

Sermet, Vincent. *Musique soul et funk en France, Histoire et Cultures de 1960 a nos jours*. Thesis, Université de Marne-la-Vallée, directed by Sylvie Dallet, 2006.

Seton-Watson, Hugh. *The East European Revolution*. London: Methuen, 1950.

Shiller, Robert J. "La nouvelle lutte des classes." *Le Monde économie*, VI, 6 février 2007.

Siller, Javier Perez, ed. *La Découverte de l' Amérique? Les regards sur l'autre à travers les manuels scolaires*. Paris: L'Harmattan-Georg Eckert Institut, 1992. Preface by Marc Ferro, foreword by Rainer Riemeschneider.

Simmel, Georg. *Le Conflit*. Paris: Circé Poche, 2000–2003.

Stern, Fritz. *Dreams and Disillusions. National Socialism in the Drama of the German Past*. New York: Vintage, 1989.

Stern, Fritz. *The Politics of Cultural Despair. A Study in the Rise of the Germanic Ideology.* Berkeley: University of California Press, 1974.

Sternhell, Zeev. *Ni droite ni gauche, l'idéologie fasciste en France.* Paris: NiL 2000.

Stora, Benjamin. *La Guerre invisible, Algérie, années 90.* Paris: Presses des Sciences-Politiques, 2001.

Suffert, Georges. "Crise dans l'armée." *Esprit*, mai 1957, pp. 819–20.

Tackett, Timothy. *Par la volonté du peuple. Comment les députés de 1789 sont devenus révolutionnaires.* Paris: Albin Michel, 1996.

Toynbee, Arnold J. *An Historian's Approach to Religion.* Oxford: Oxford University Press, 1956.

Vermeil, Edmond. *Doctrinaires de la révolution allemande, 1918–1938.* Paris: Sorlot, 1939.

Veyne, Paul. *Le Pain et le cirque.* Paris: Seuil, 1975.

Veyne, Paul. *Quand notre monde est devenu chrétien (312–394).* Paris: Albin Michel, 2007.

Viatteau, Alexandra. *Katyn, l'armée polonaise assassinée.* Paris: Éditions Complexe, 1982.

Vuckovic, Nadja. "Qui demande des réparations et pour quels crimes?" In Marc Ferro, *Le Livre noir du colonialisme, XVIe–Xxe siècle: de l'extermination à la repentance*, pp. 762–787. Paris: R. Laffont, 2001.

Weil, François. *Histoire de New York.* Paris: Fayard, 2000.

Weil, Patrick. *La France et ses étrangers, 1938–1991.* Paris: Calmann-Lévy, 1991.

Werth, Nicolas. "Un Etat contre son peuple." In *Le Livre noir du communisme*, ed. Stéphane Courtois. Paris: Laffont, 1997, pp. 49–299.

Wieviorka, Michel. *Sociétés et terrorisme.* Paris: Fayard, 1998.

Winock, Michel. *La France et les Juifs.* Paris: Seuil, 2004.

Yassine, Abdelsalam. *Islamiser la modernité.* Paris: Al Ofok, 1998.

Yonnet, Paul. "Rock, Pop, Punk, Masques et Vertiges du peuple adolescent." *Le Débat*, 25 mai 1983, pp. 133–56.

Yonnet, Paul. *Voyage au centre du malaise français, l'antiracisme et le roman national.* Paris: Gallimard, 1993.

Zarka, Yves-Charles. "l'Islam en France." In Yves-Charles Zarka, Sylvia Taussig, and Cynthia Fleury, *Cites.* Paris: PUF, 2004. (See also the articles by Olivier Roy, Giles Kepel, and Alexandre Adler.)

Zeghal, Malika. *Gardiens de l'Islam, les oulemas d'Al Azhar.* Paris: Presses des Sciences-Politiques, 1996.

Zerner, Monique. "Hérésies." In Le Goff-Schmitt, pp. 464–81.

Zunz, Olivier. *Le Siècle américain.* Paris: Fayard, 2000.

Index